The Early Years ABC, Numbers, Shapes, & Letter Tracing

This book belongs to:

_ _

_ _

_ _

unicorn
LEARNING GROUP

Note to Parents

This is a beginning numbers, shapes, and letters tracing book that helps young children learn in an easy and fun way. By the tender age of three, many children can hold a crayon and scribble on paper.

This practice book is designed to help your child develop the skills of pen control, shapes, number recognition, and ABCs, which are among the first milestones in their education journey. It is organized into five (5) sections that are aligned with common core state standards for pre-VPK through Kindergarten. It contains progressive skills building on each other for kids to develop the confidence to read and write.

Part 1:
- Pen Control- Begin tracing with lines and curves as well as simple fun pictures.

Part 2:
- Learning the Alphabet- Trace and pattern letters (A-Z, a-z)
- Color pictures

Part 3:
- Trace the numbers 1-10
- Color the pictures

Part 4:
- Shapes Recognition- Tracing basic shapes and items found around the home and school
- Color the shapes

Part 5:
- Introducing 15 pre-primer words for children to recognize and practice writing

By working through this book your child will create a foundation for the future. They will strengthen their little finger muscles through coloring, tracing, and writing, gain exposure to the ABCs, numbers 1-10, and learn the first 15 pre-primer words that will begin their reading journey.

This book requires guidance from a parent, teacher, or caregiver to aid in a child's practice in the early learning education years.

You can photocopy parts of this book for use with your class, a family member, or for other personal use. However, please do not reproduce this book for an entire school or commercial use. Kindly encourage other potential users to buy their own copies of this book!

Have questions/ concerns or want free goodies or information on new material released?

Email us at:
Unicornlearninggroup@gmail.com

Title the email " Unicorn Gems" and I will send goodies your way. Thank you!

-Unicorn Learning Group(c)

Pen control

Start at the dot. Trace the dotted line and follow the arrow as a guide.

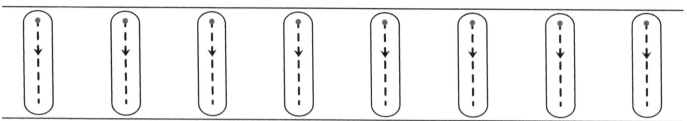

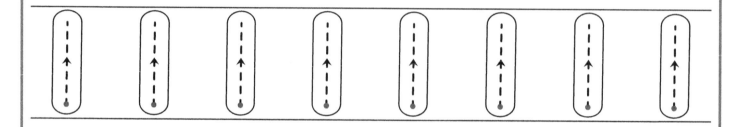

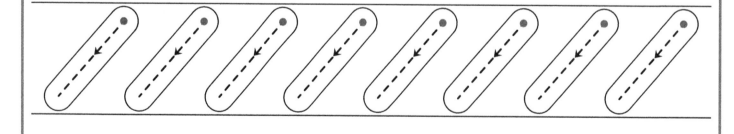

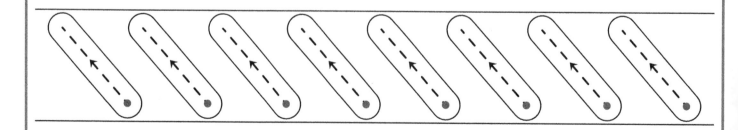

Pen control

Start at the dot. Trace the dotted line and follow the arrow as a guide.

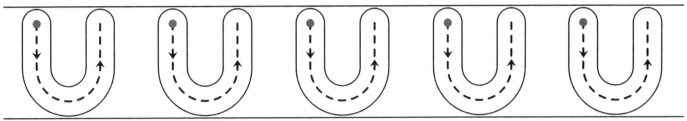

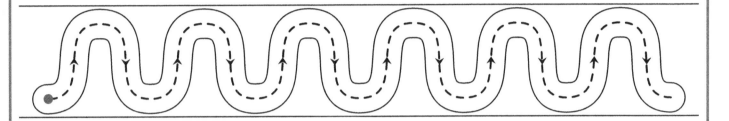

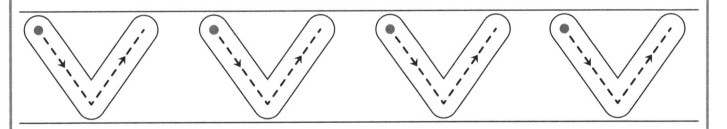

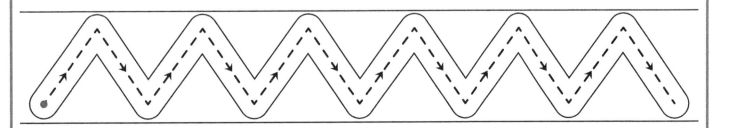

Pen control

It's a race! Help the kids get to the finish line by tracing their paths.

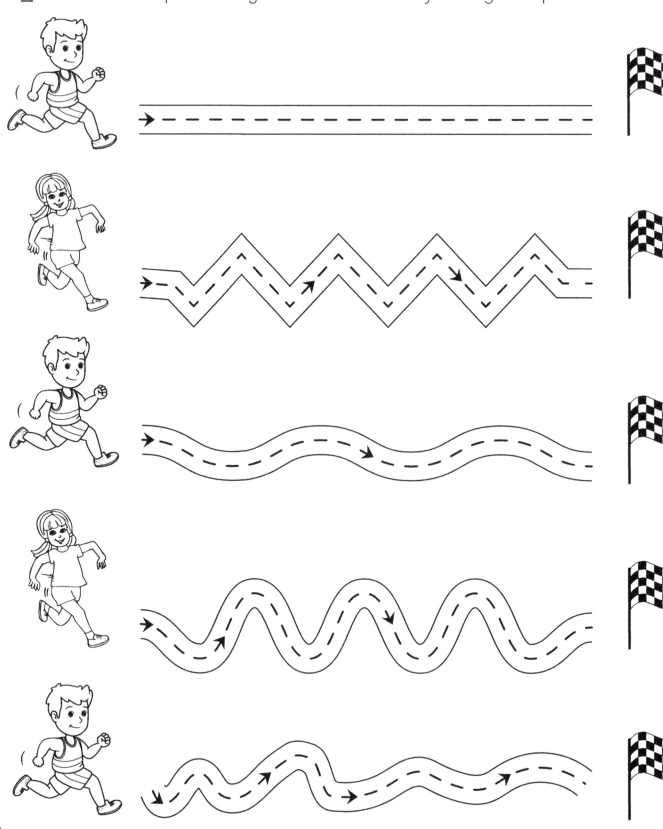

Pen control

Help the driver get home safely! Follow the arrows.

Pen control

Trace the lines to help the caterpillar and butterfly reach the fruit. Then color the pictures

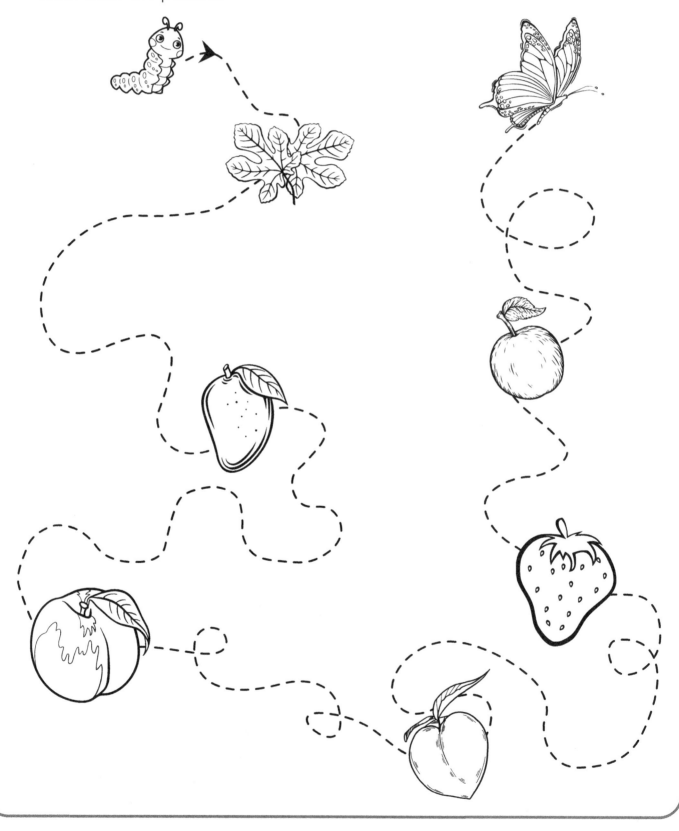

Pen control

Pen control

Pen control

Pen control

Apple

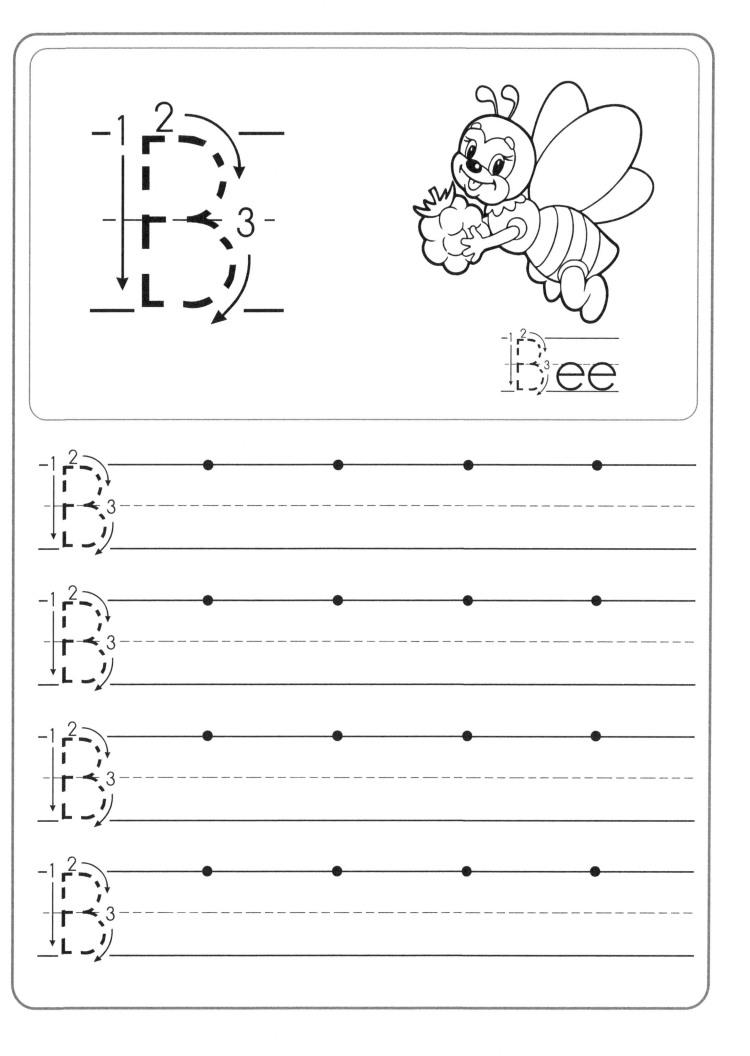

Bee

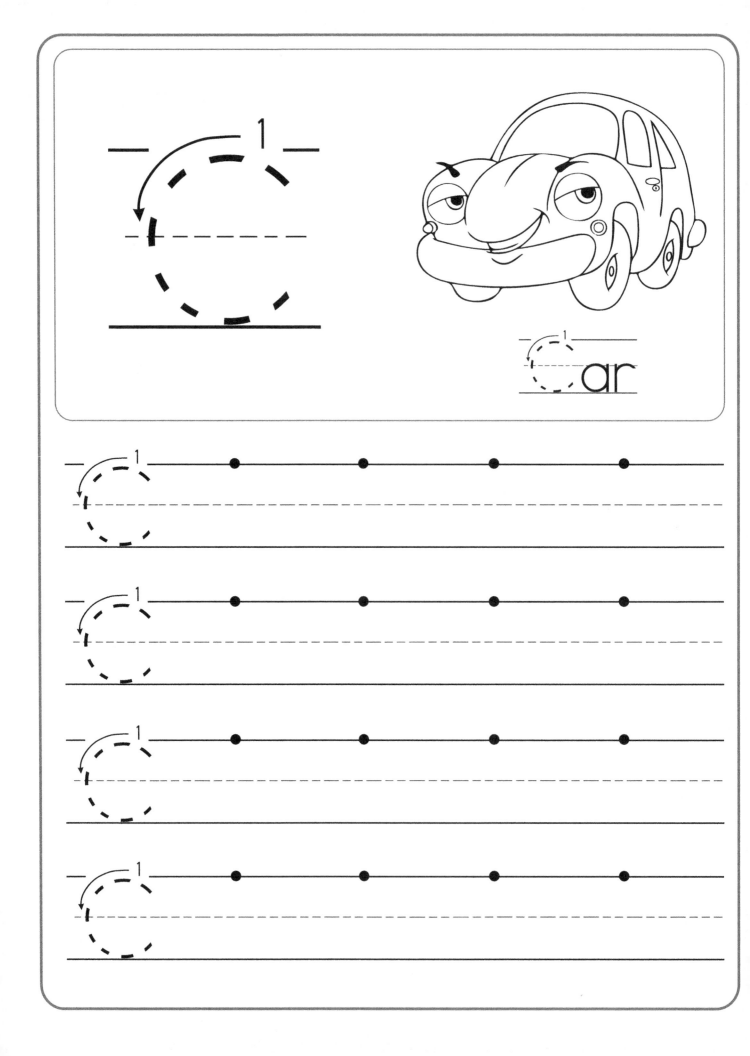

Car

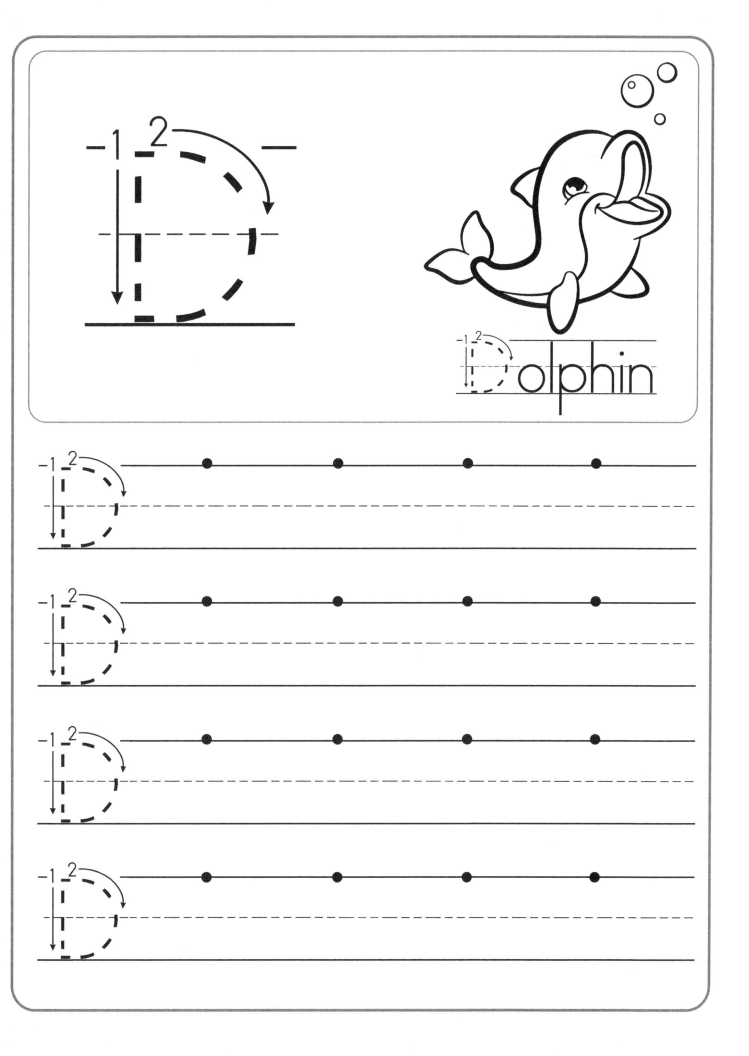

Dolphin

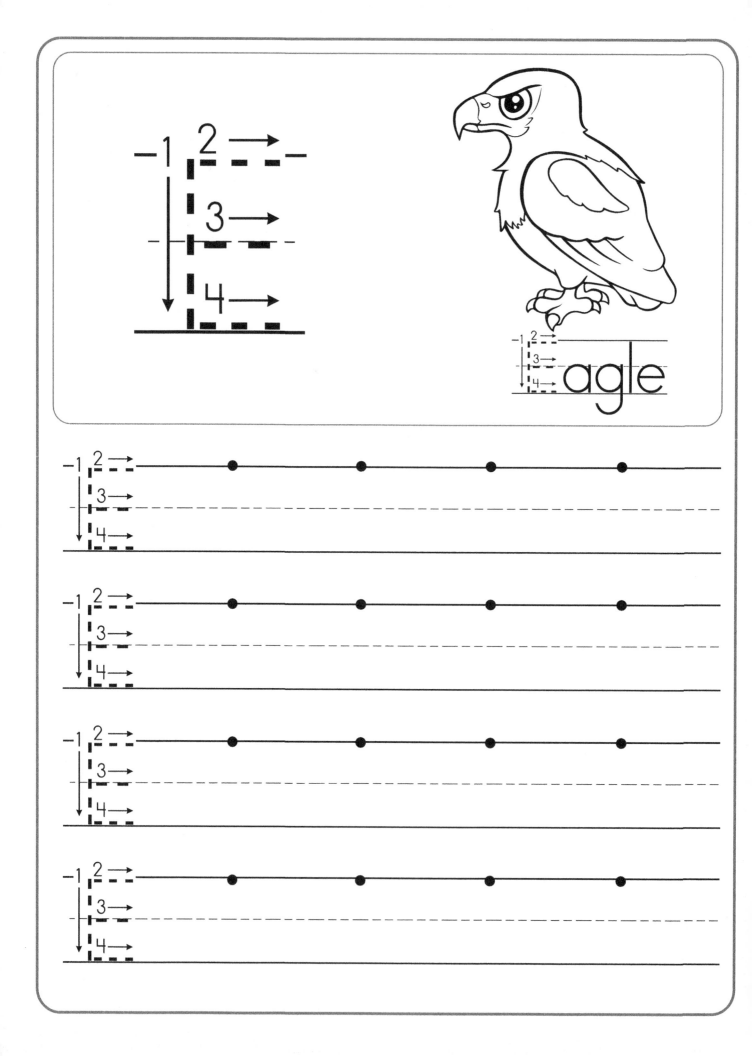

agle

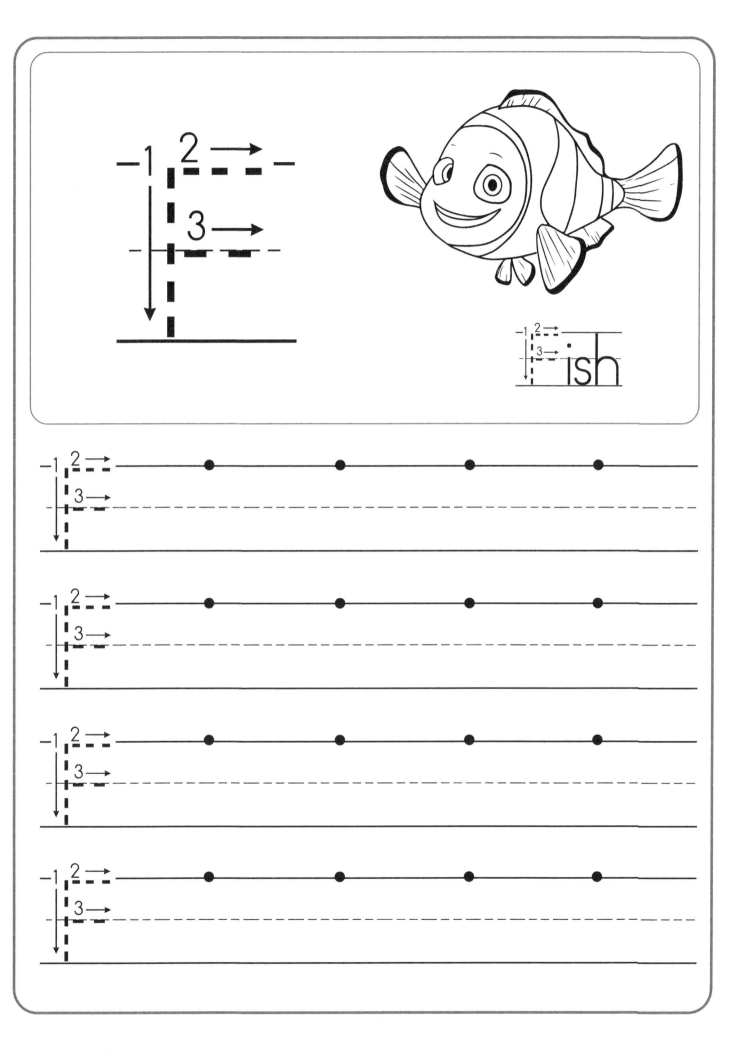

Fish

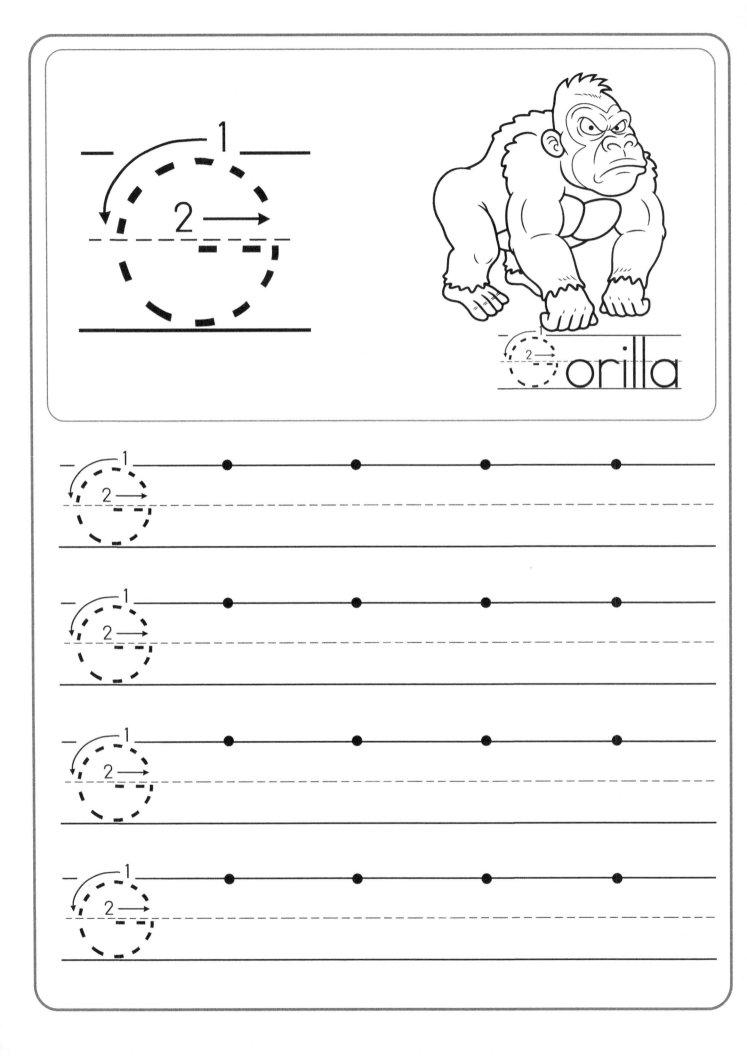

orilla

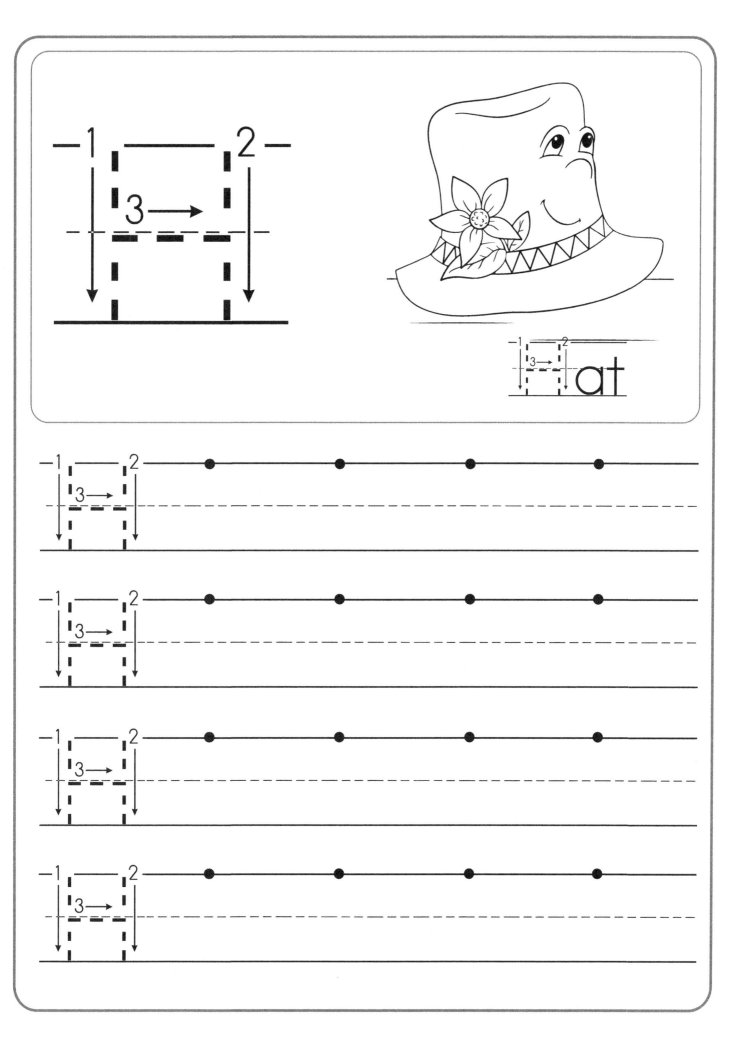

Hat

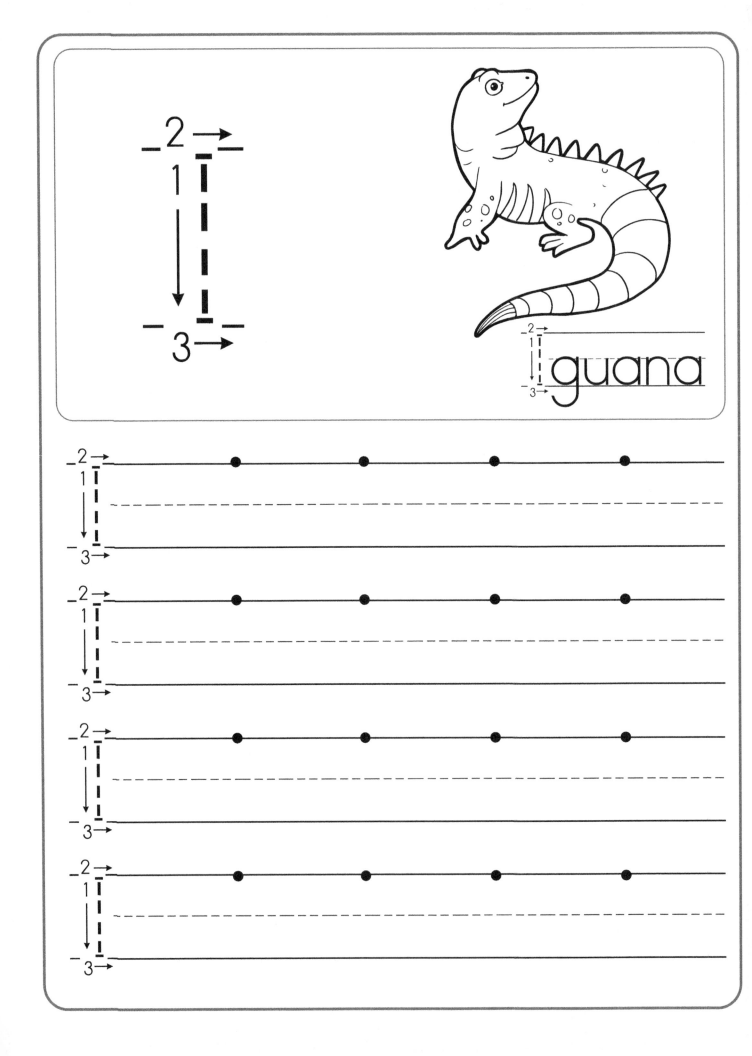

Iguana

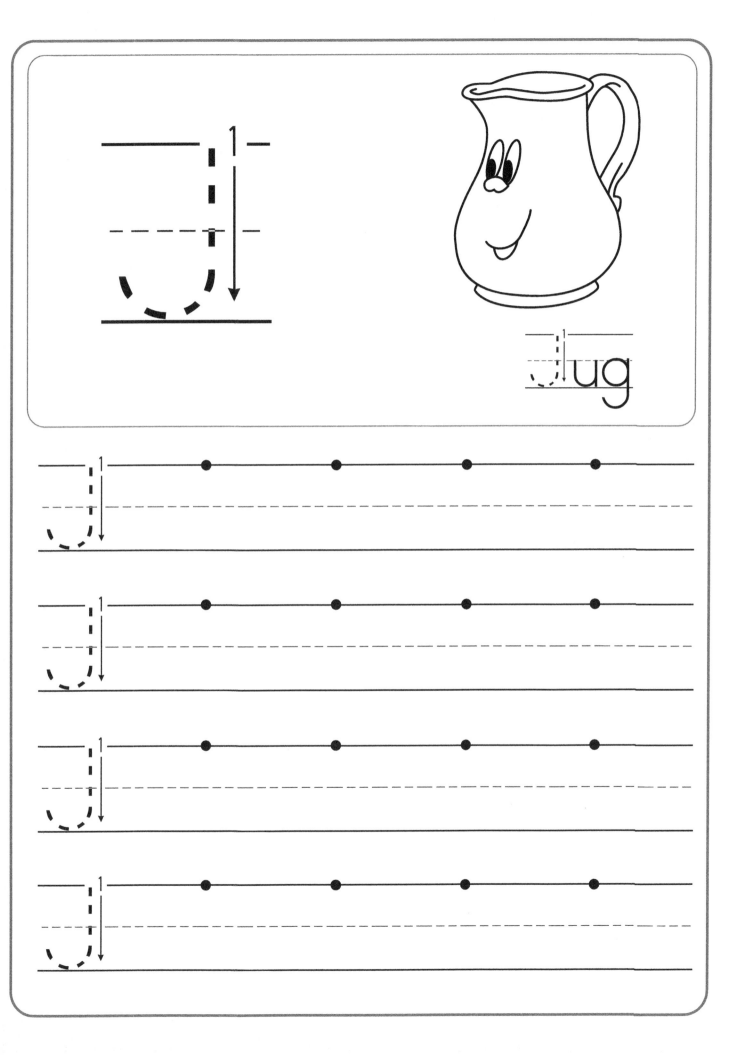

Jug

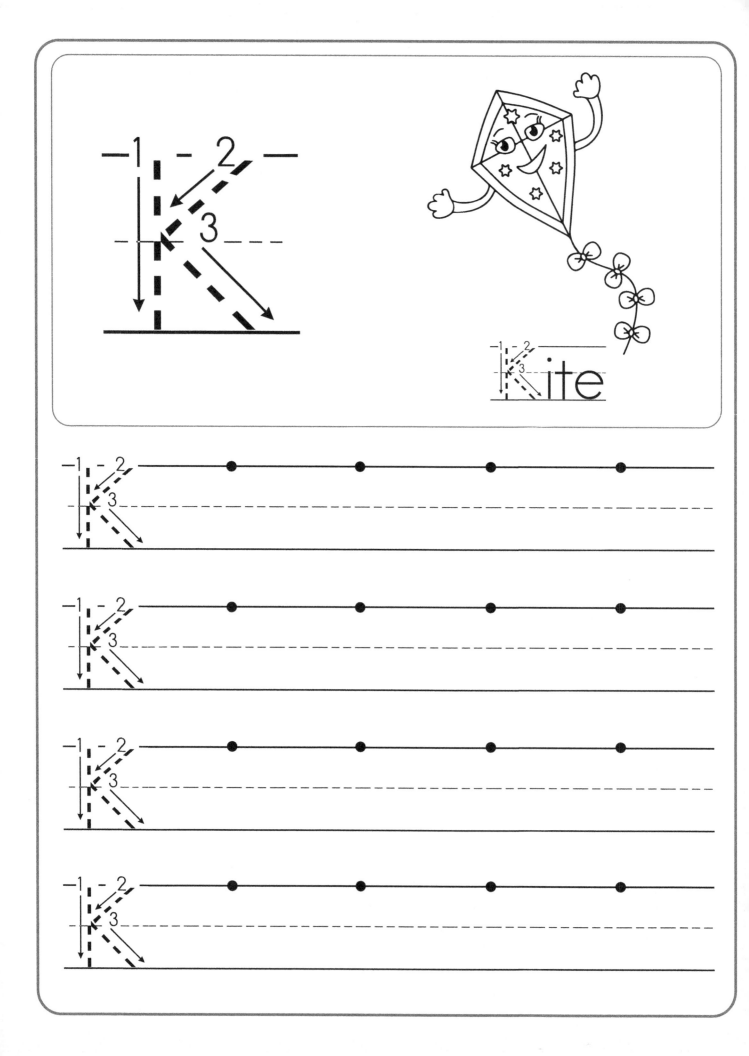

Kite

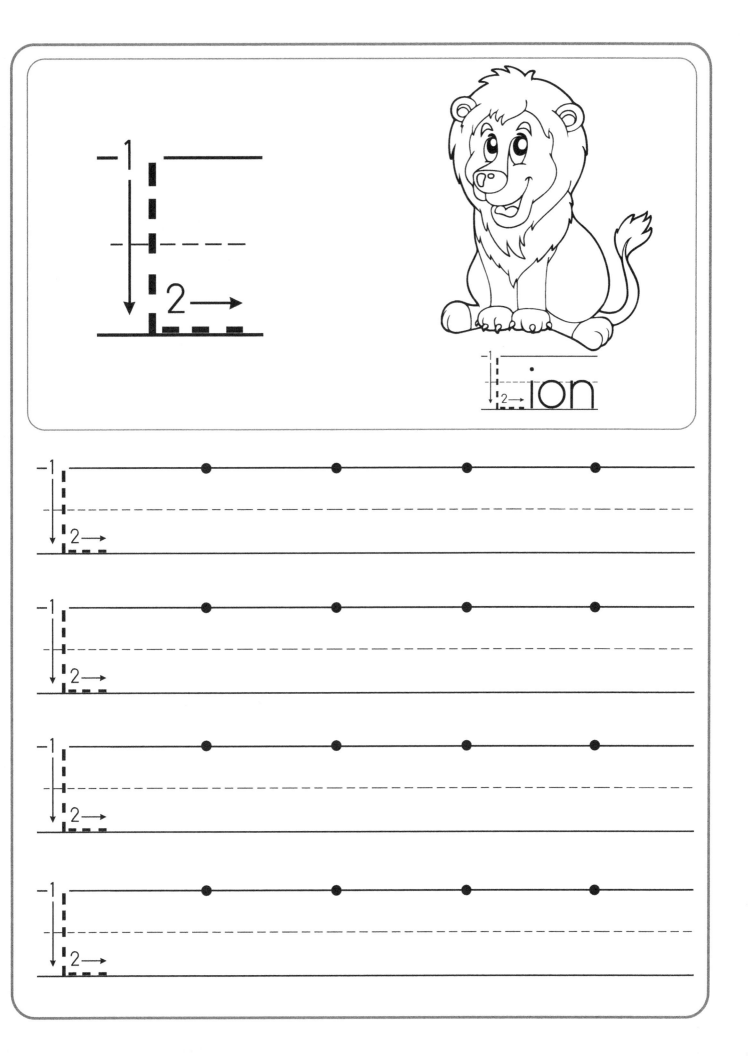

ion

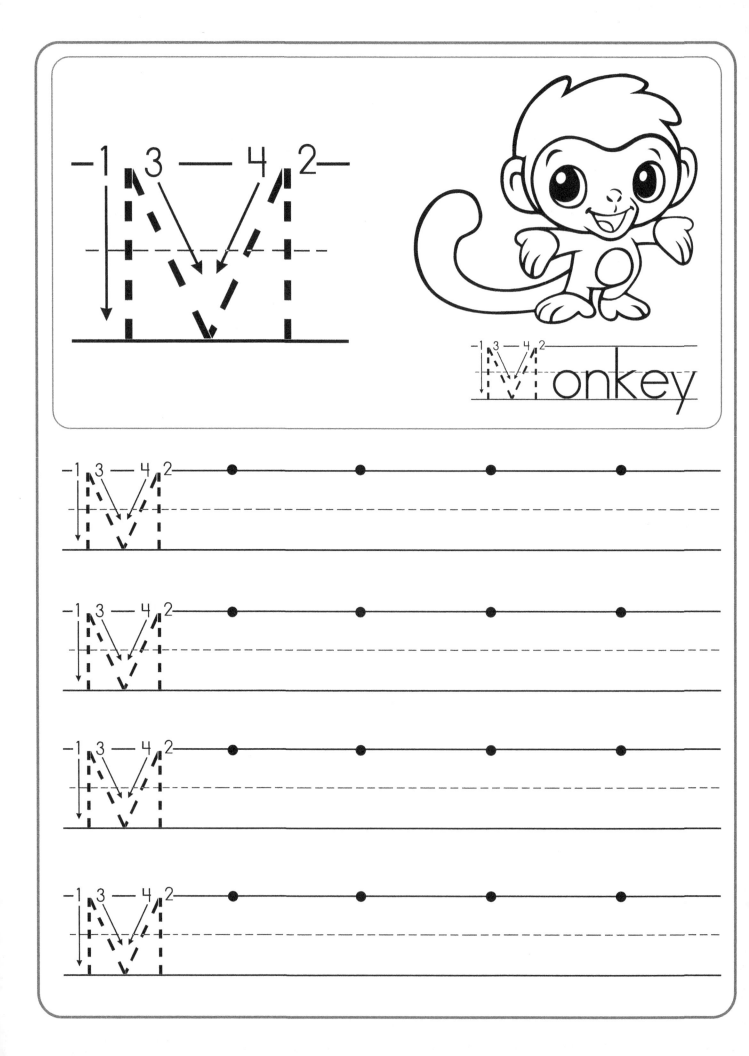

onkey

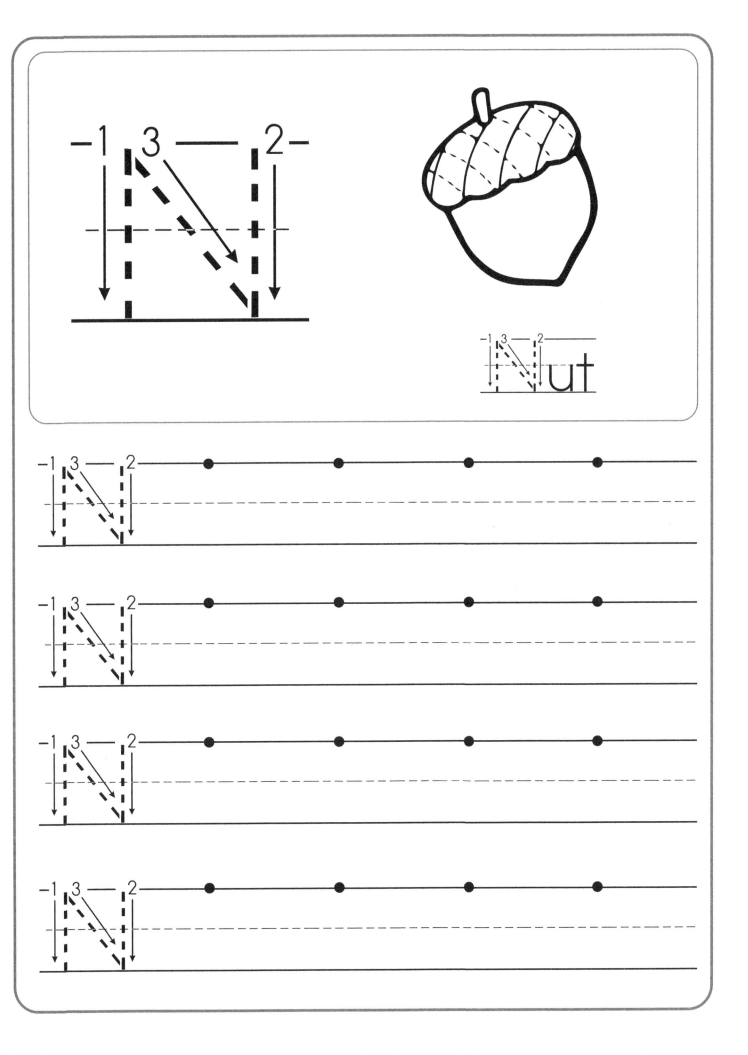

Nut

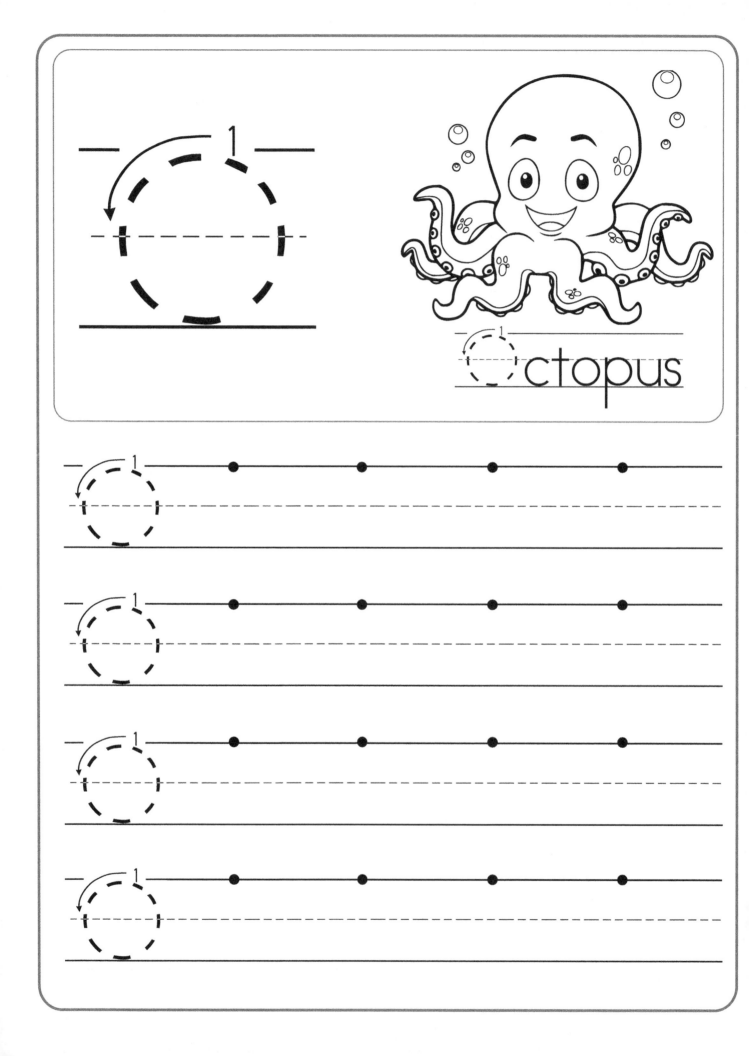

ctopus

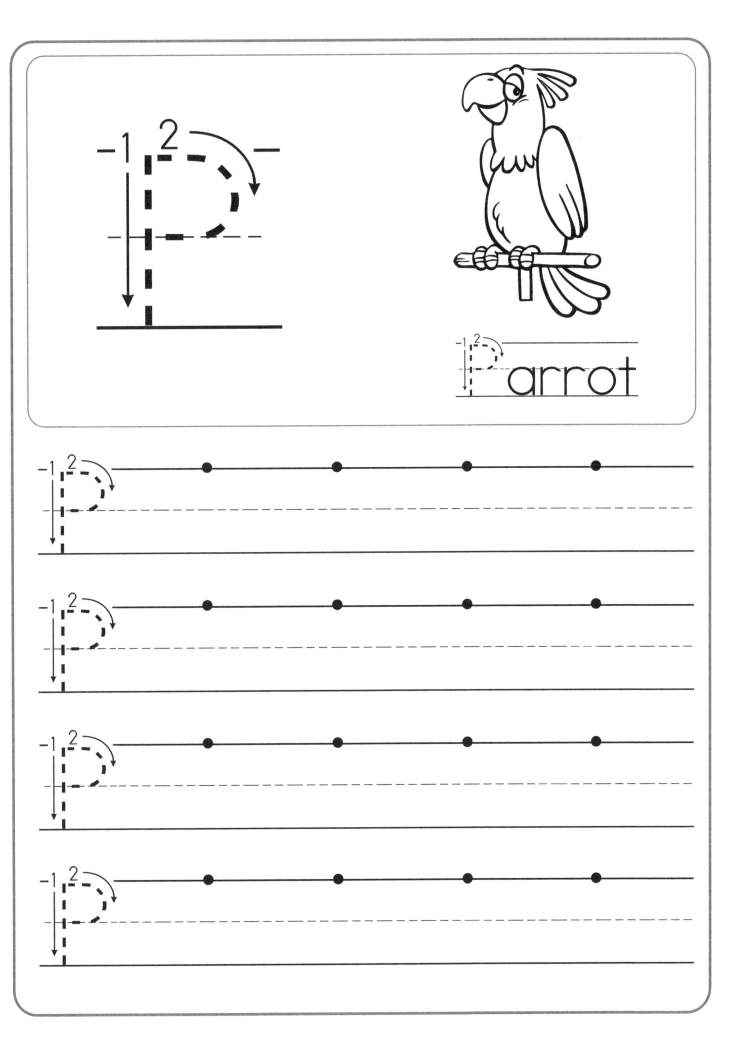

Parrot

Question mark

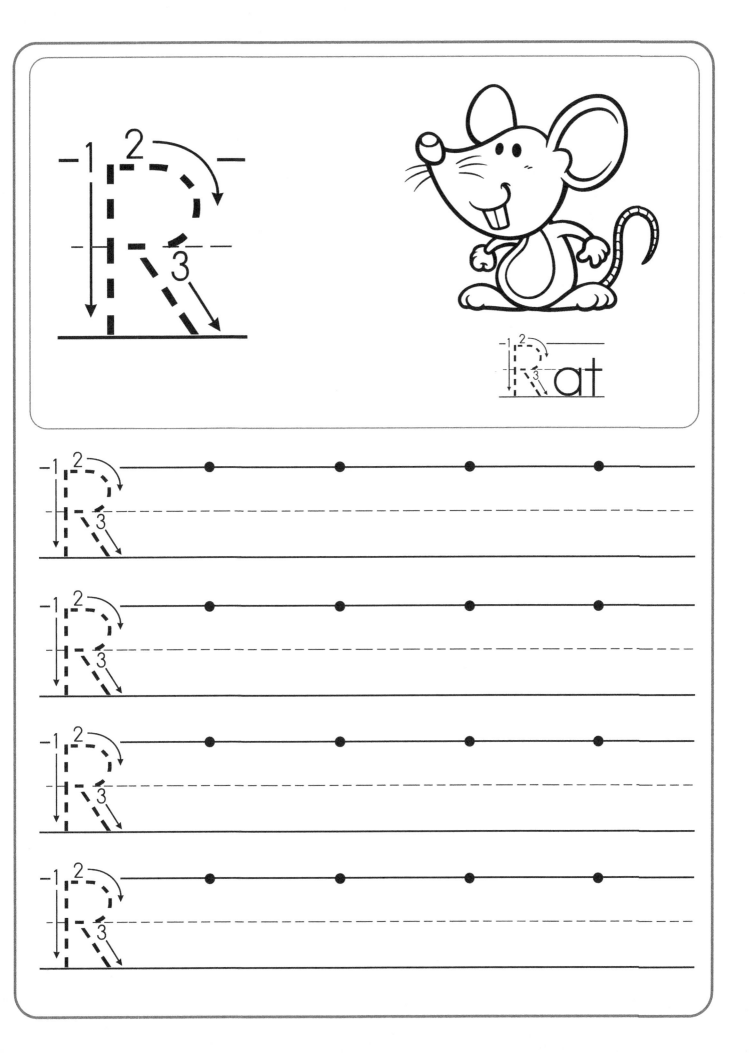

Rat

Sun

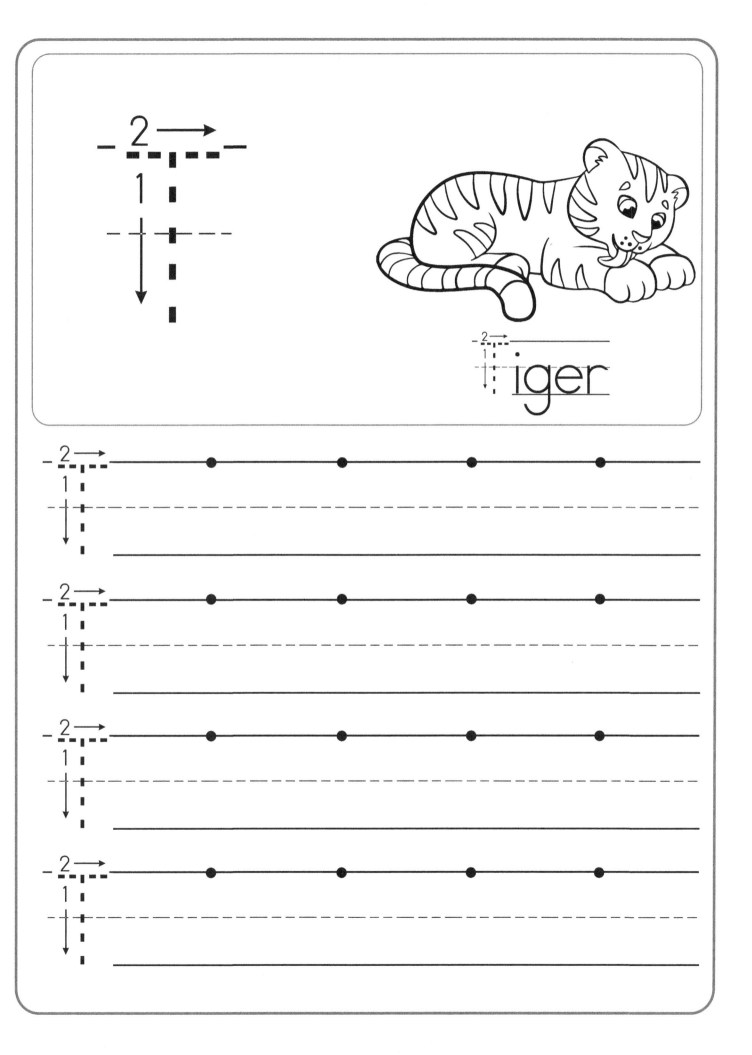

Tiger

unicorn

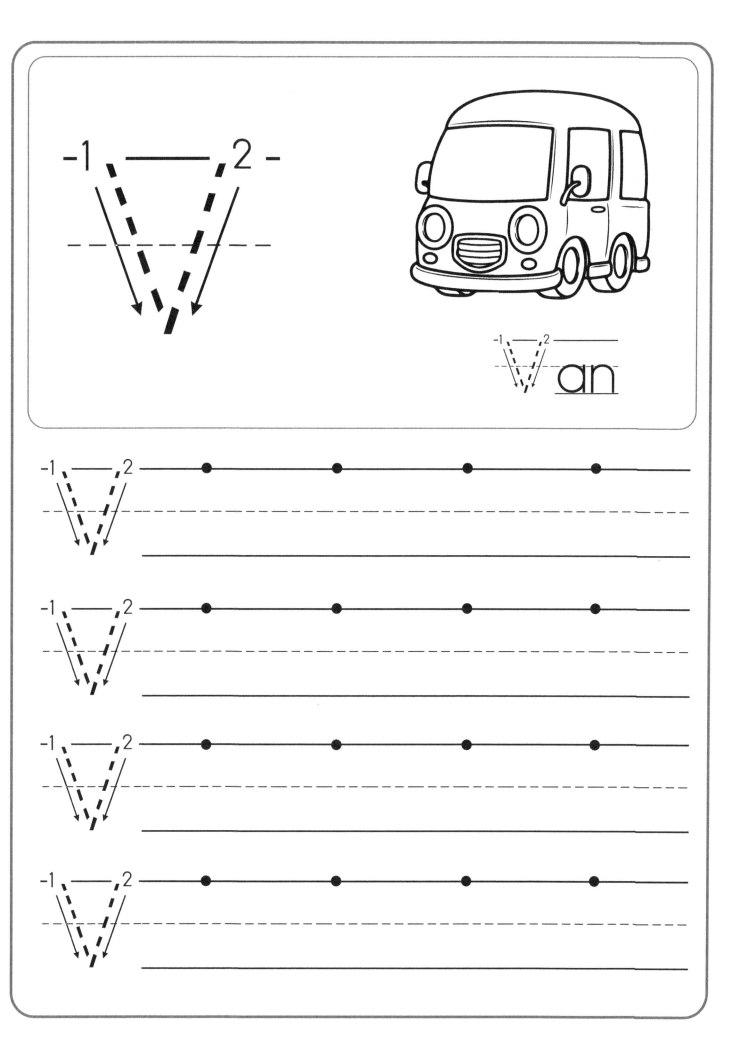

Van

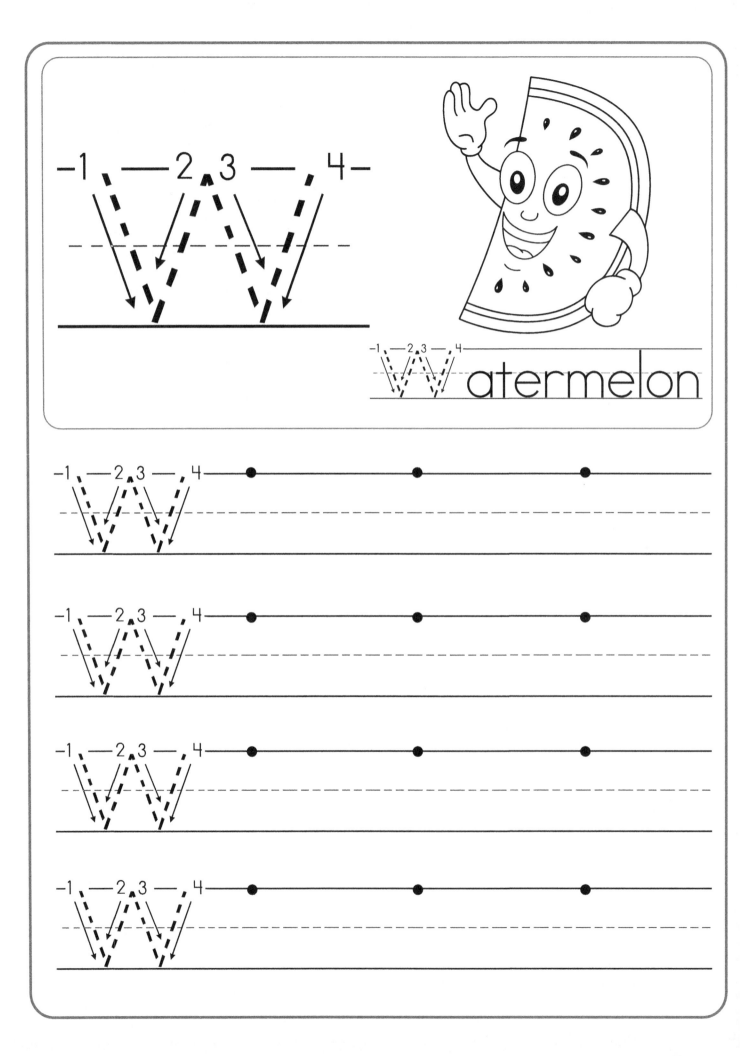

Watermelon

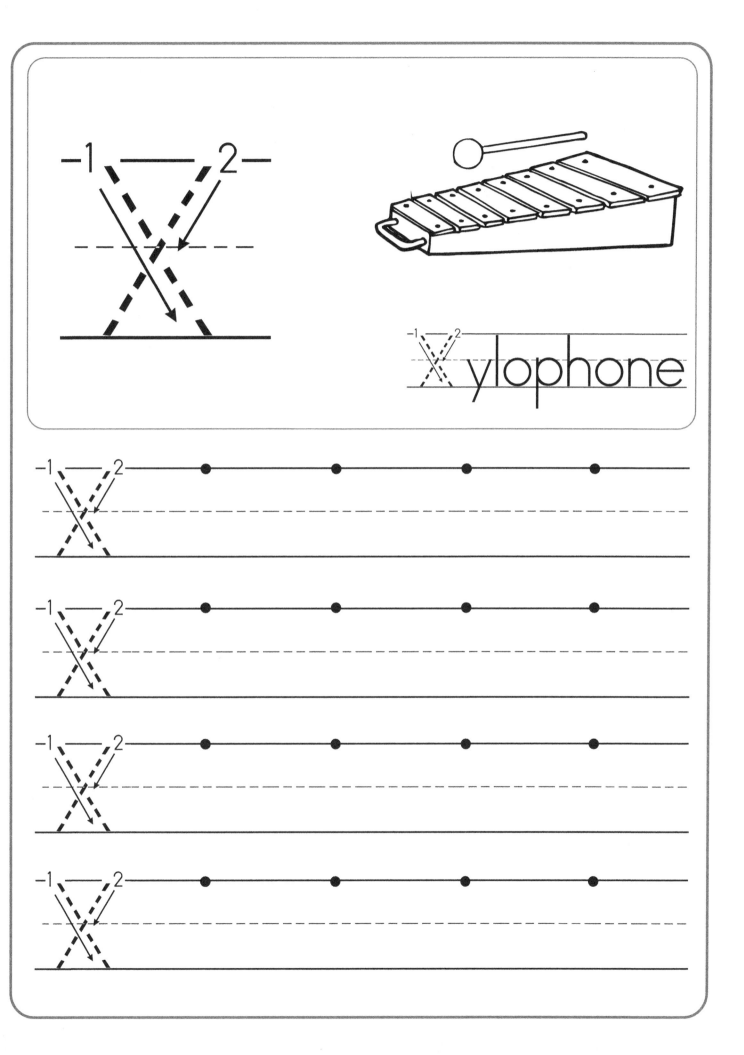

xylophone

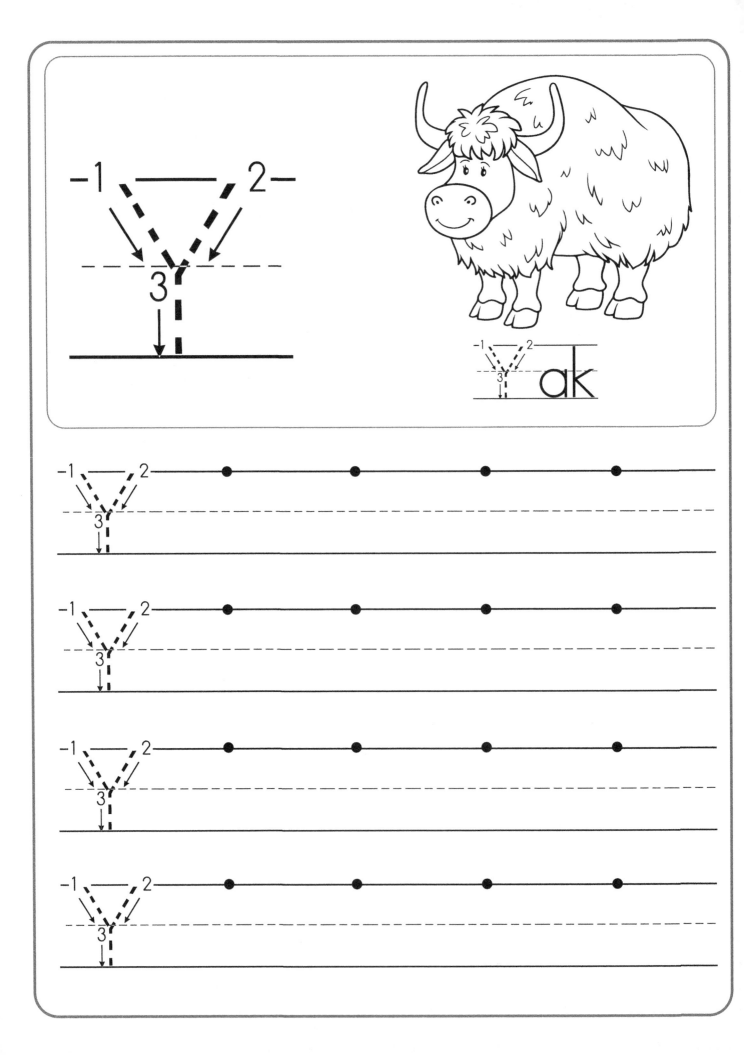

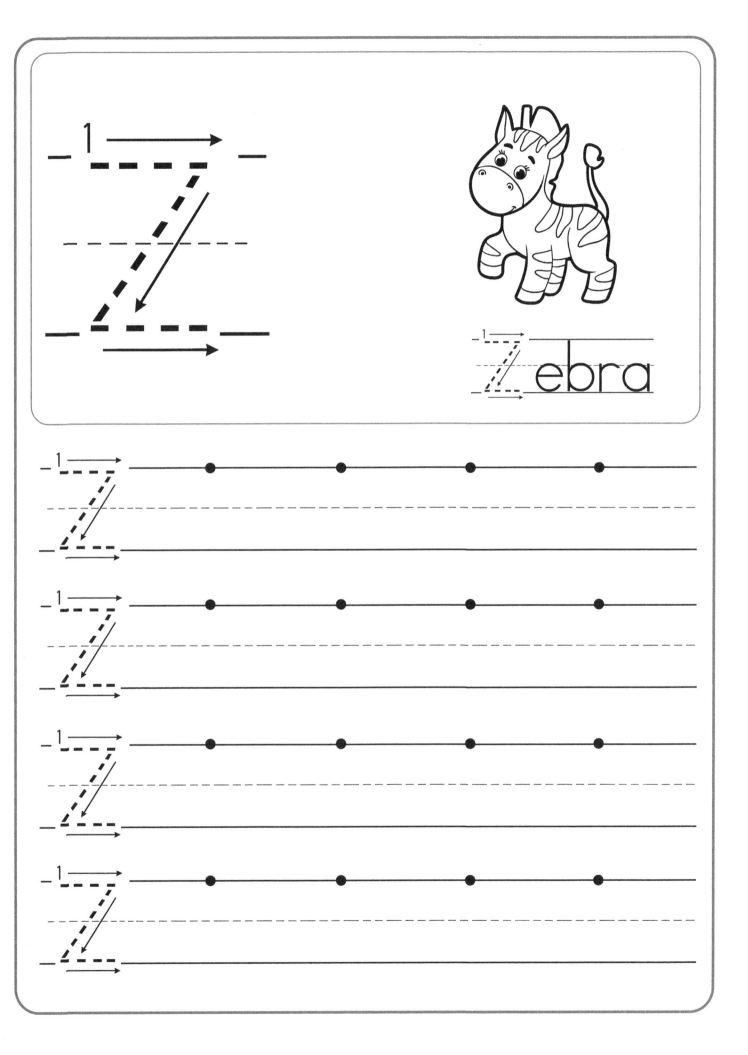

Zebra

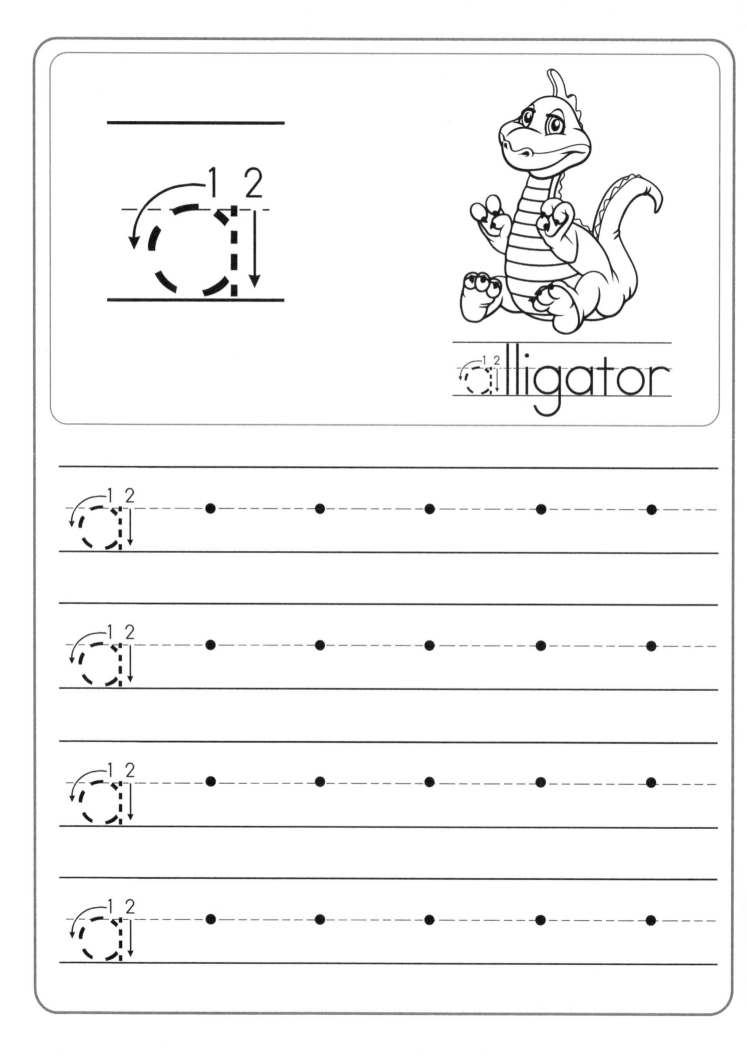

alligator

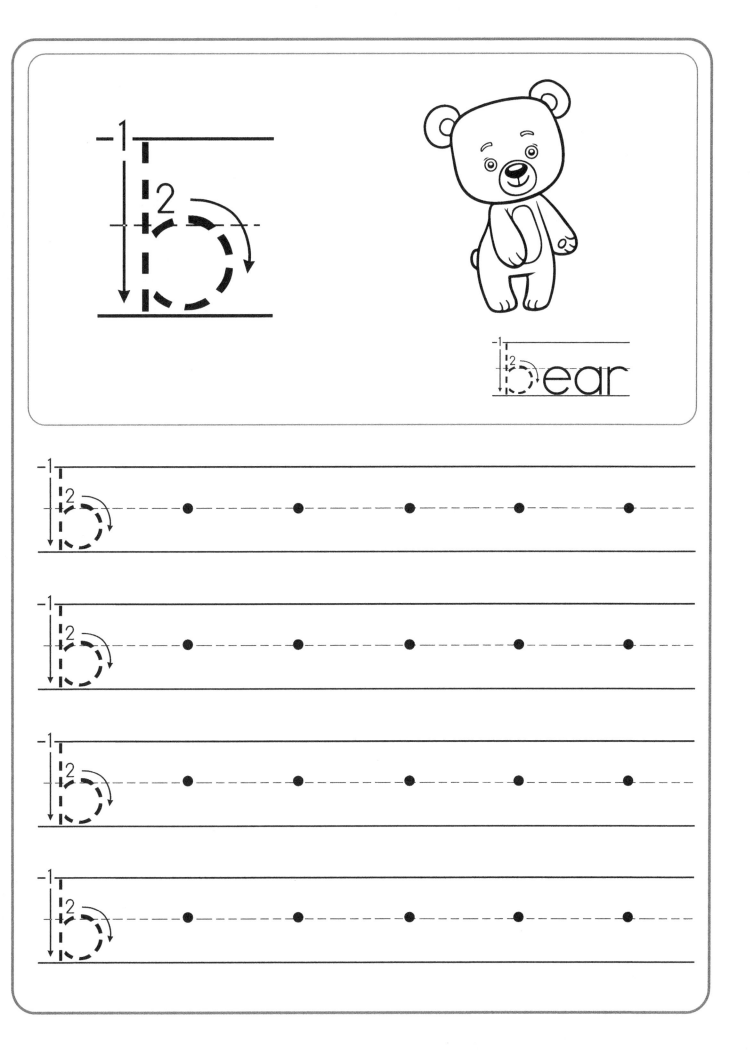

bear

cat

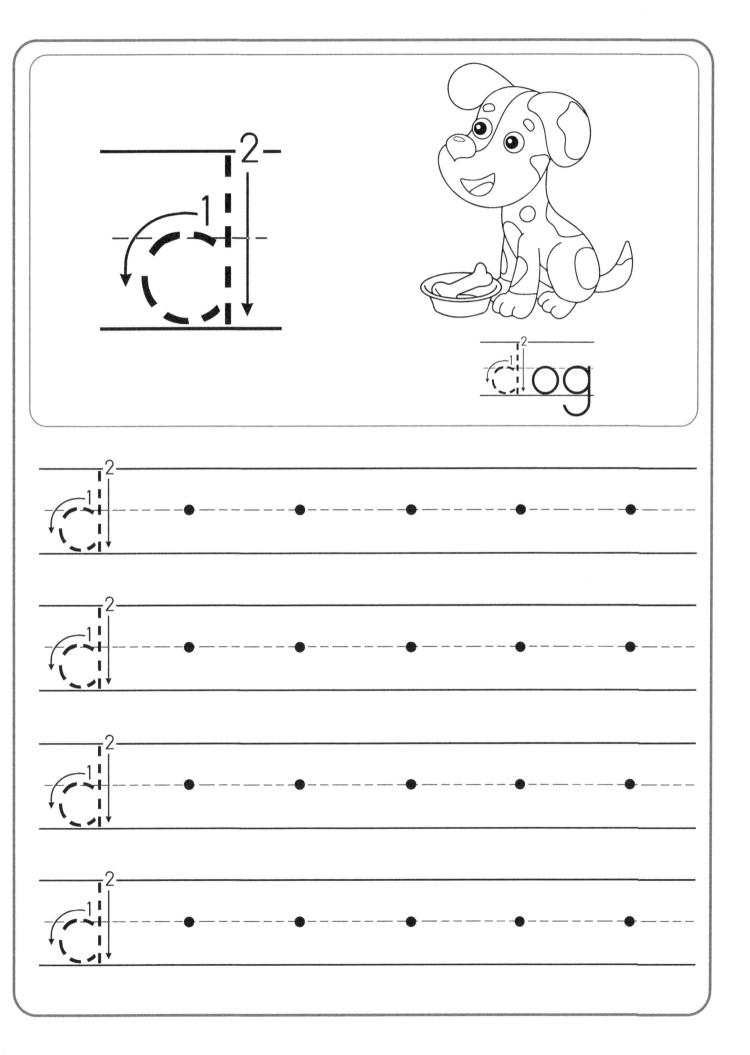

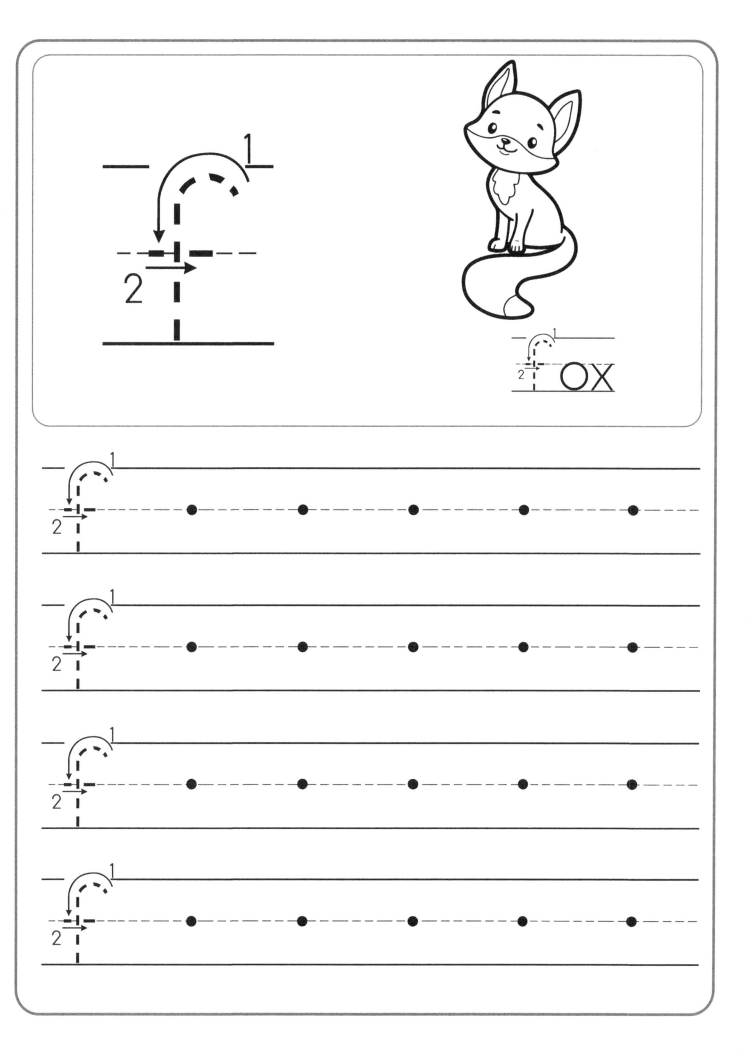

OX

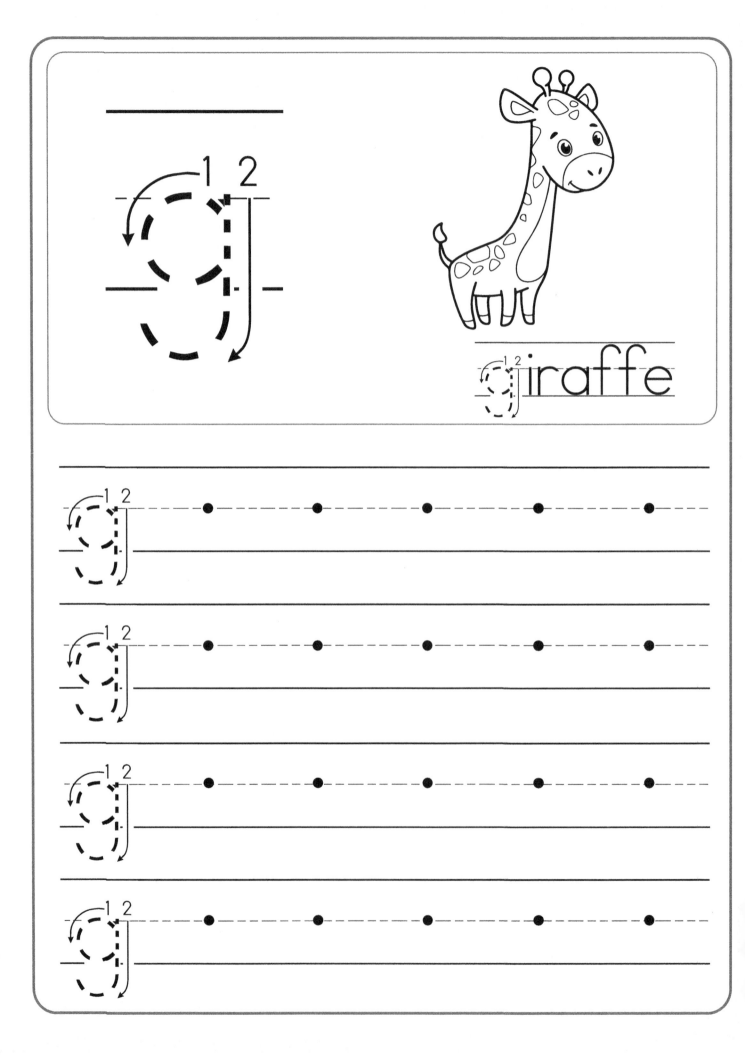

giraffe

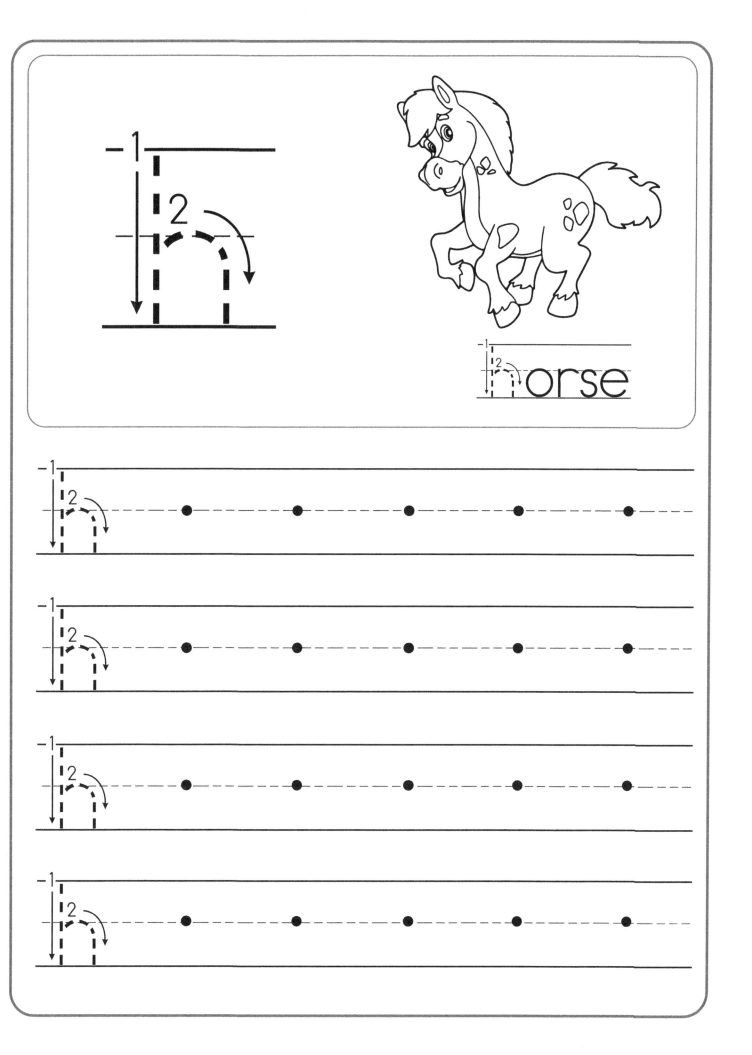

horse

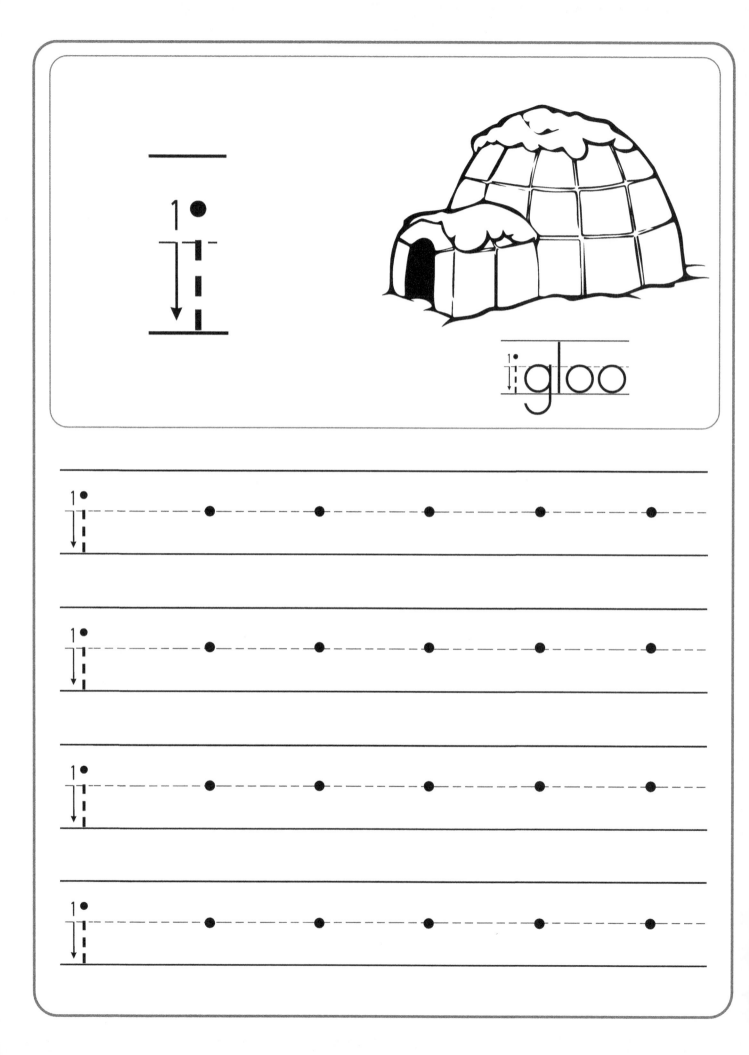

igloo

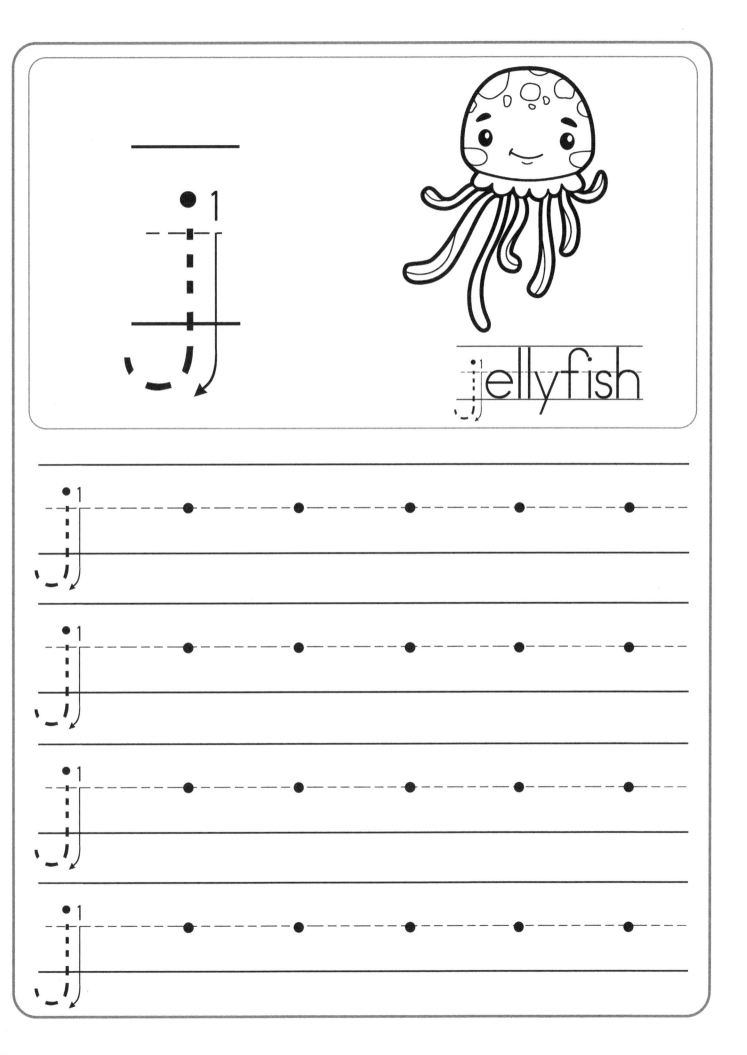

jellyfish

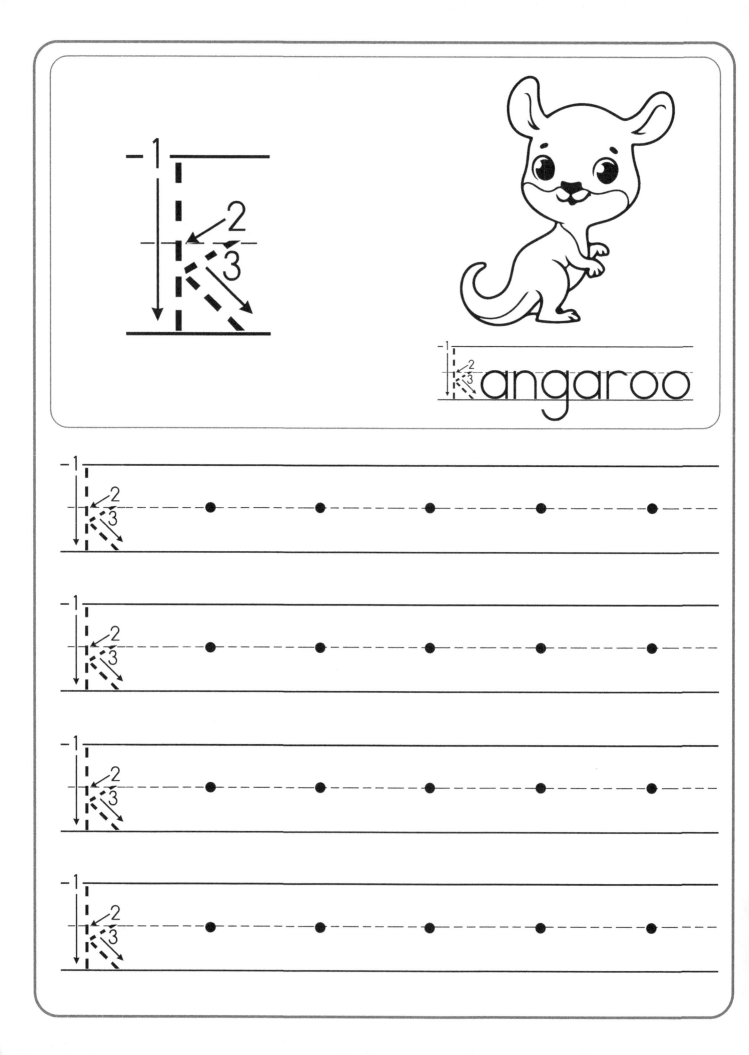

angaroo

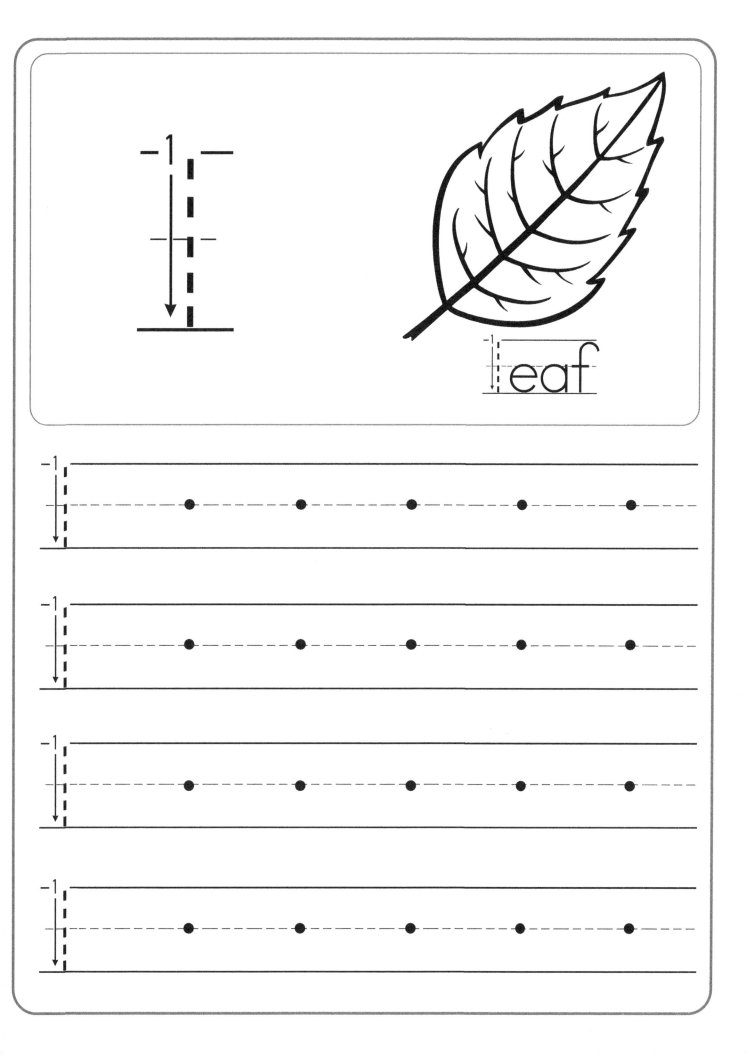

leaf

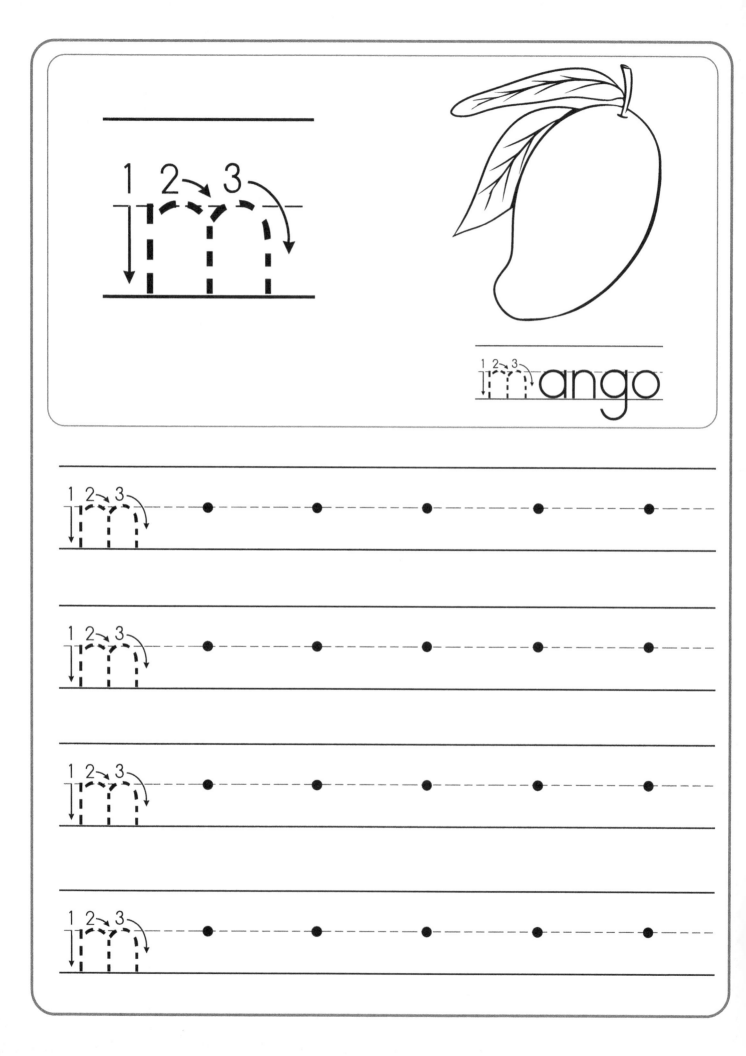

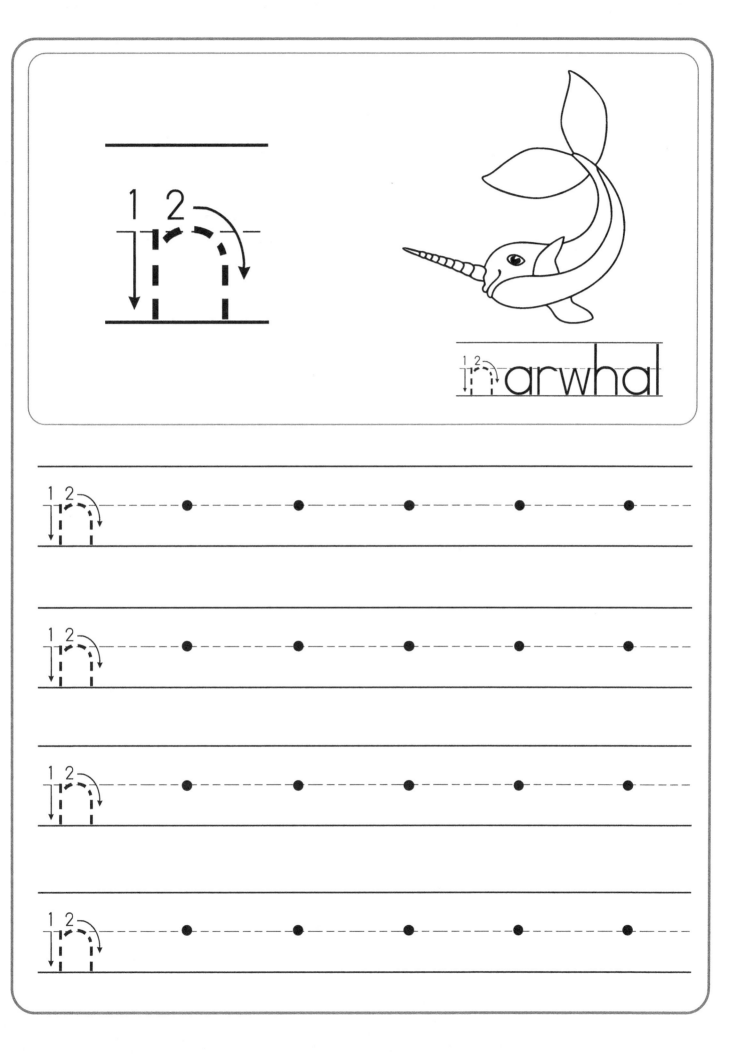

narwhal

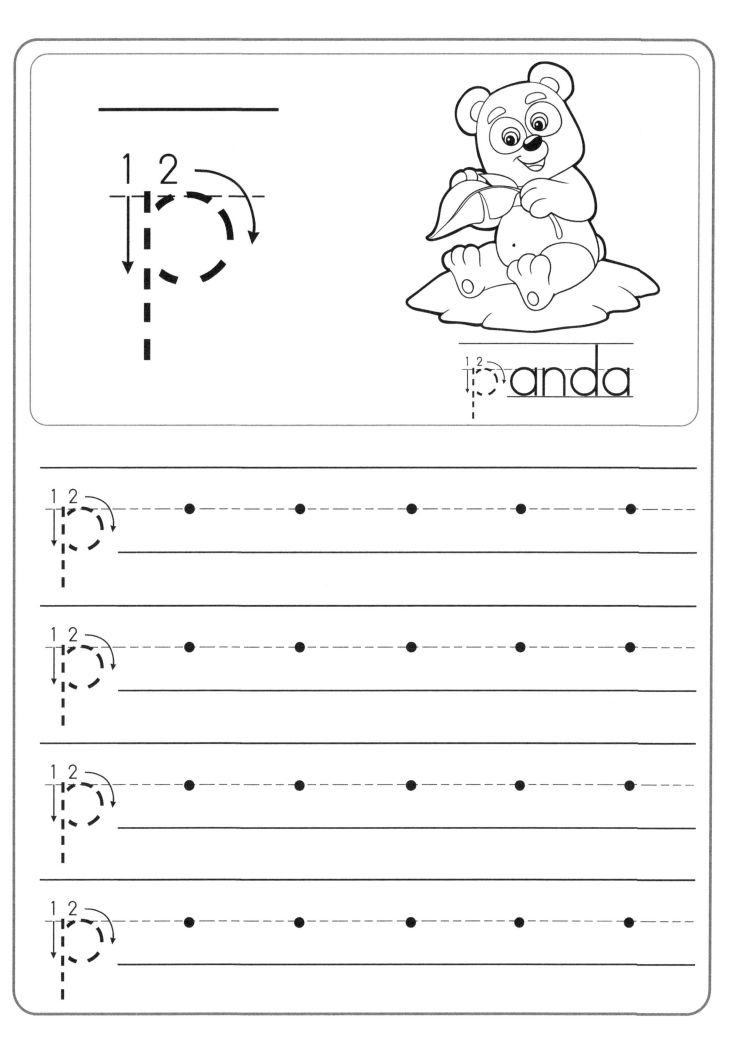

panda

quail

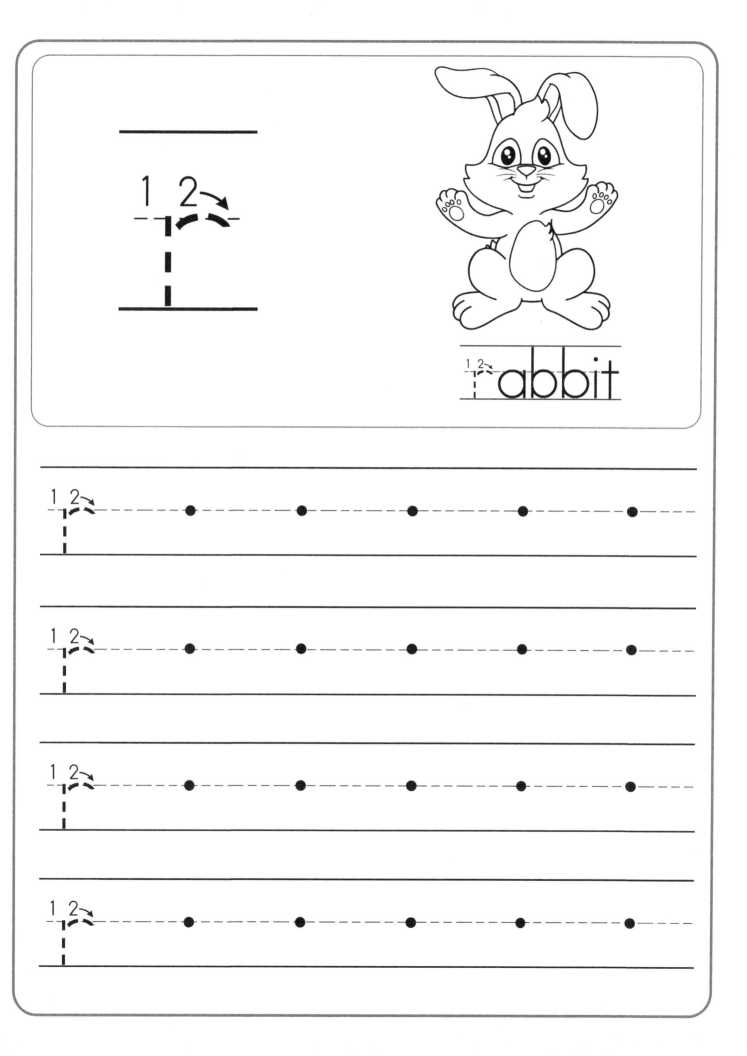

sheep

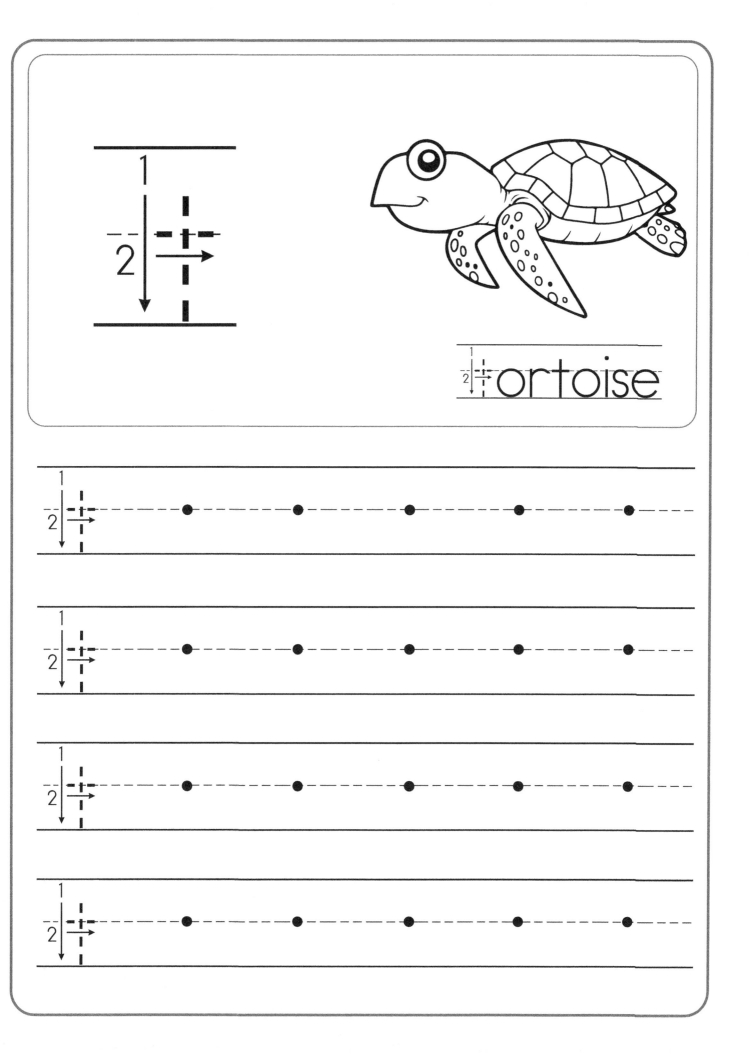

ortoise

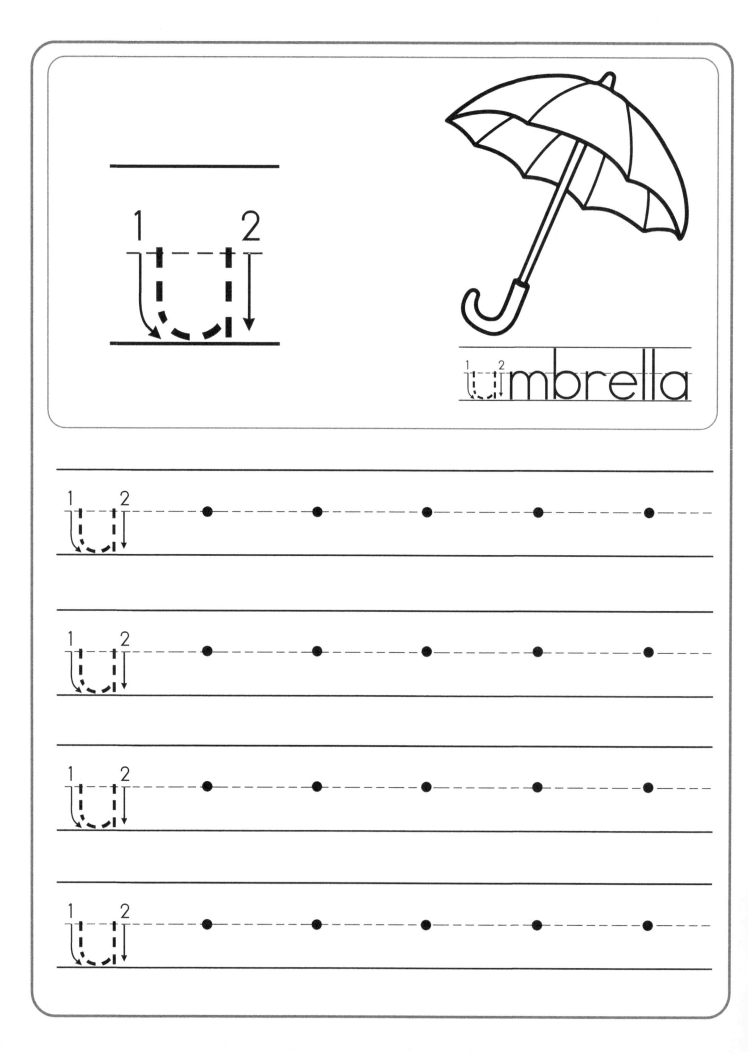

umbrella

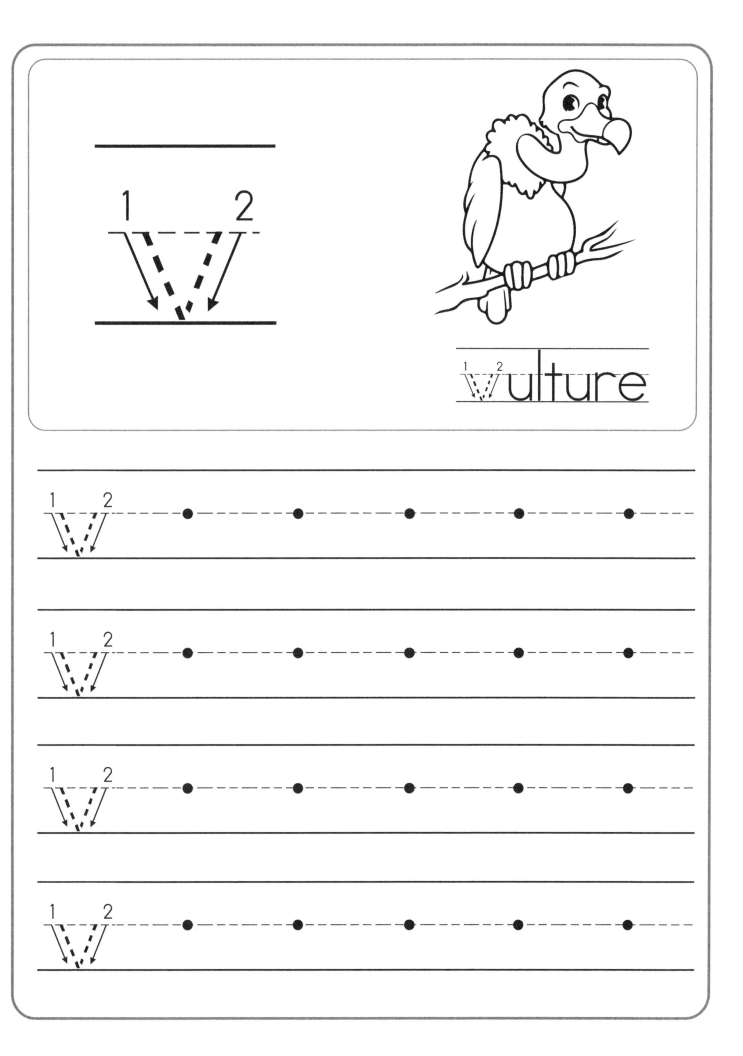

Vulture

X-ray fish

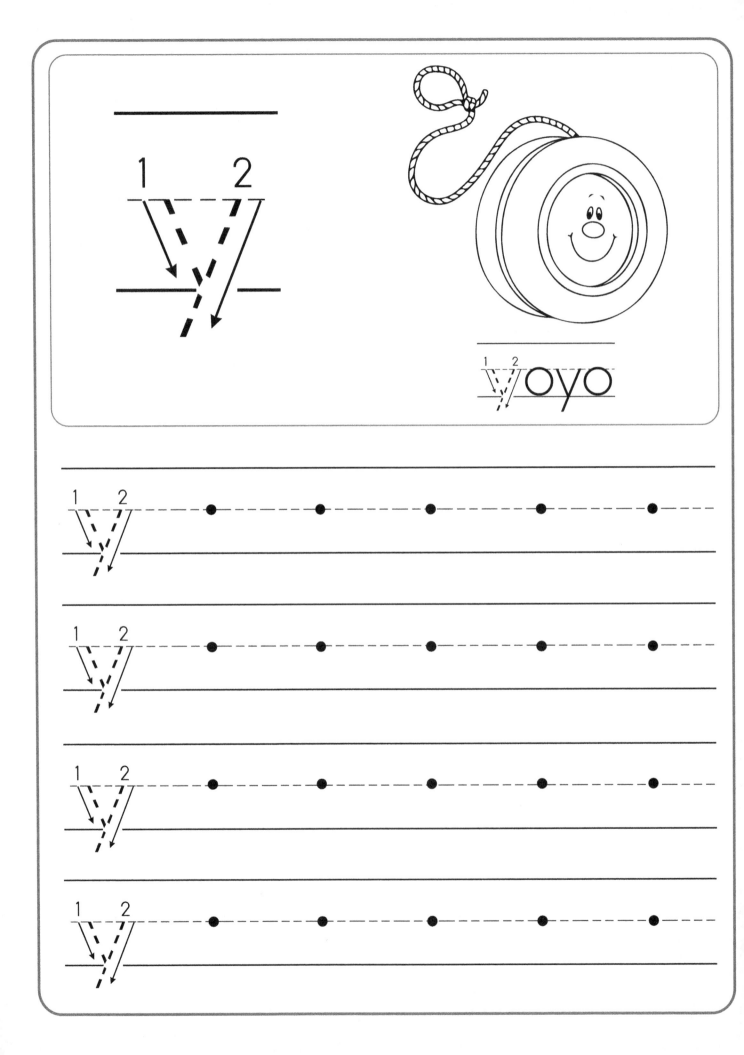

yoyo

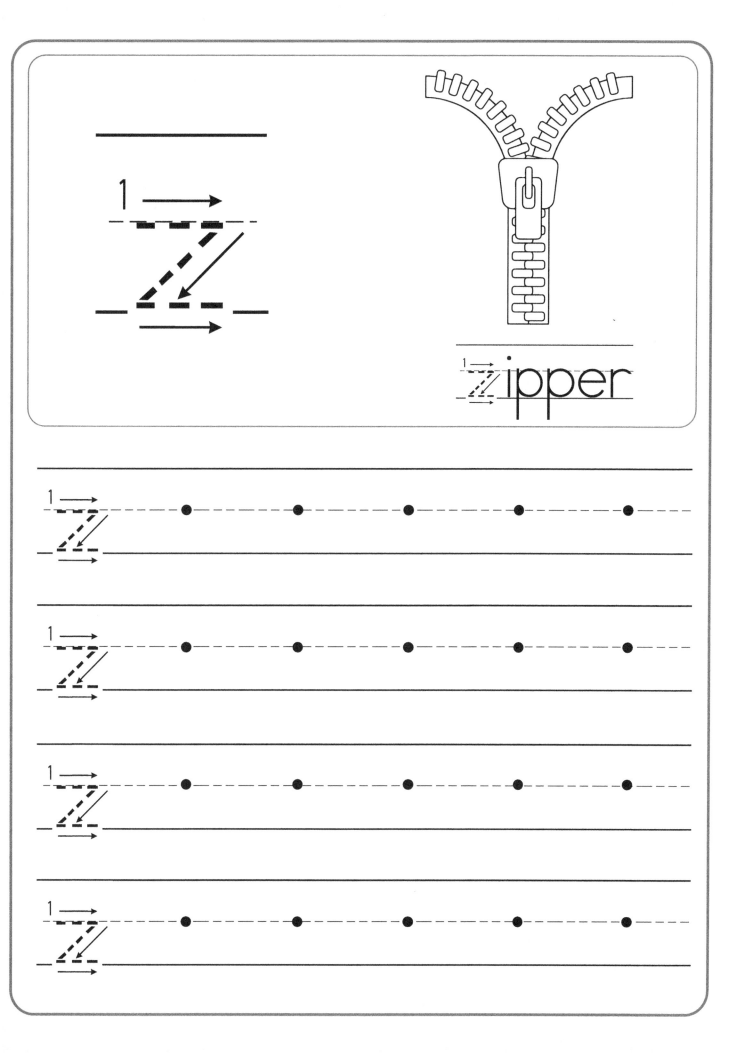

Zipper

Trace the number. Start at the 1 and follow the numbers and arrows in order. Color the pictures.

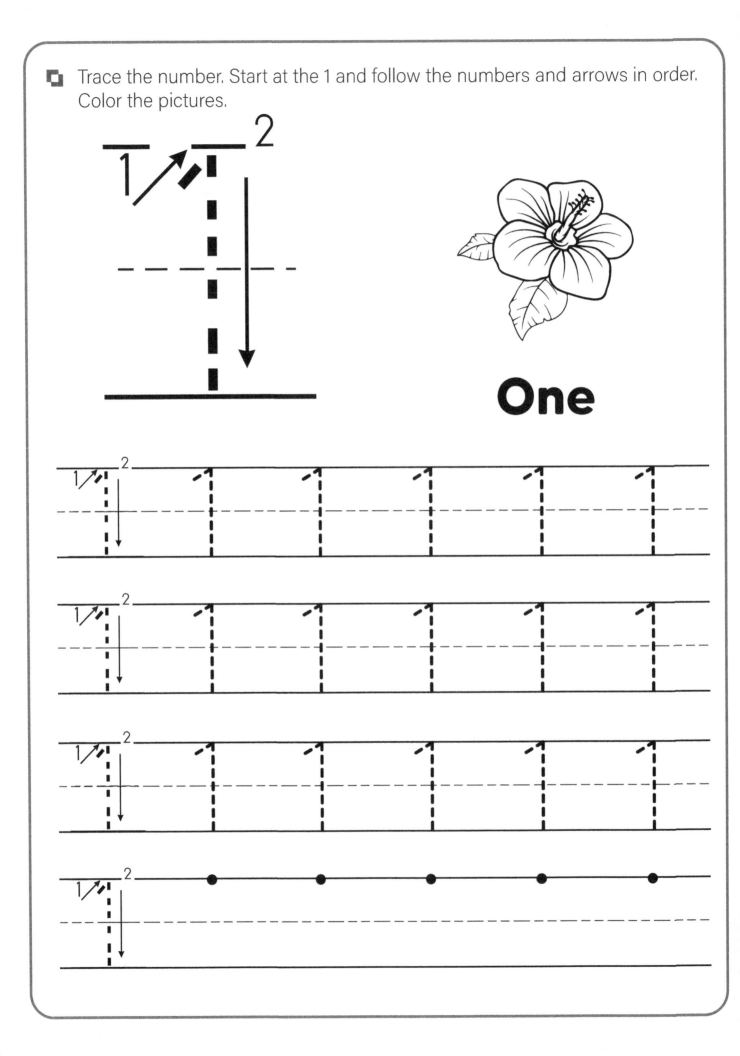

One

Trace the number. Start at the 1 and follow the numbers and arrows in order. Color the pictures.

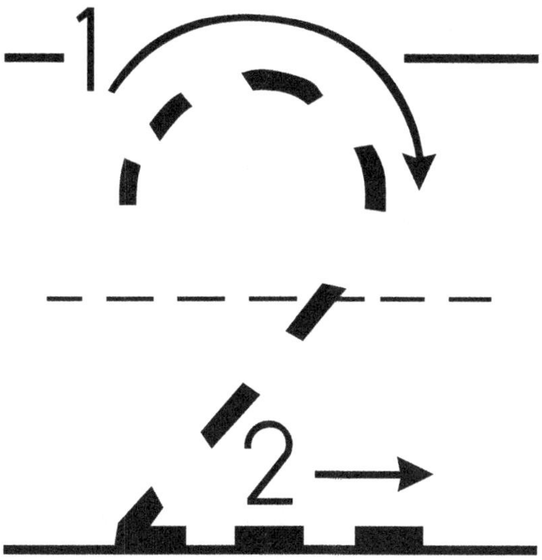

-1

$2 \rightarrow$

Two

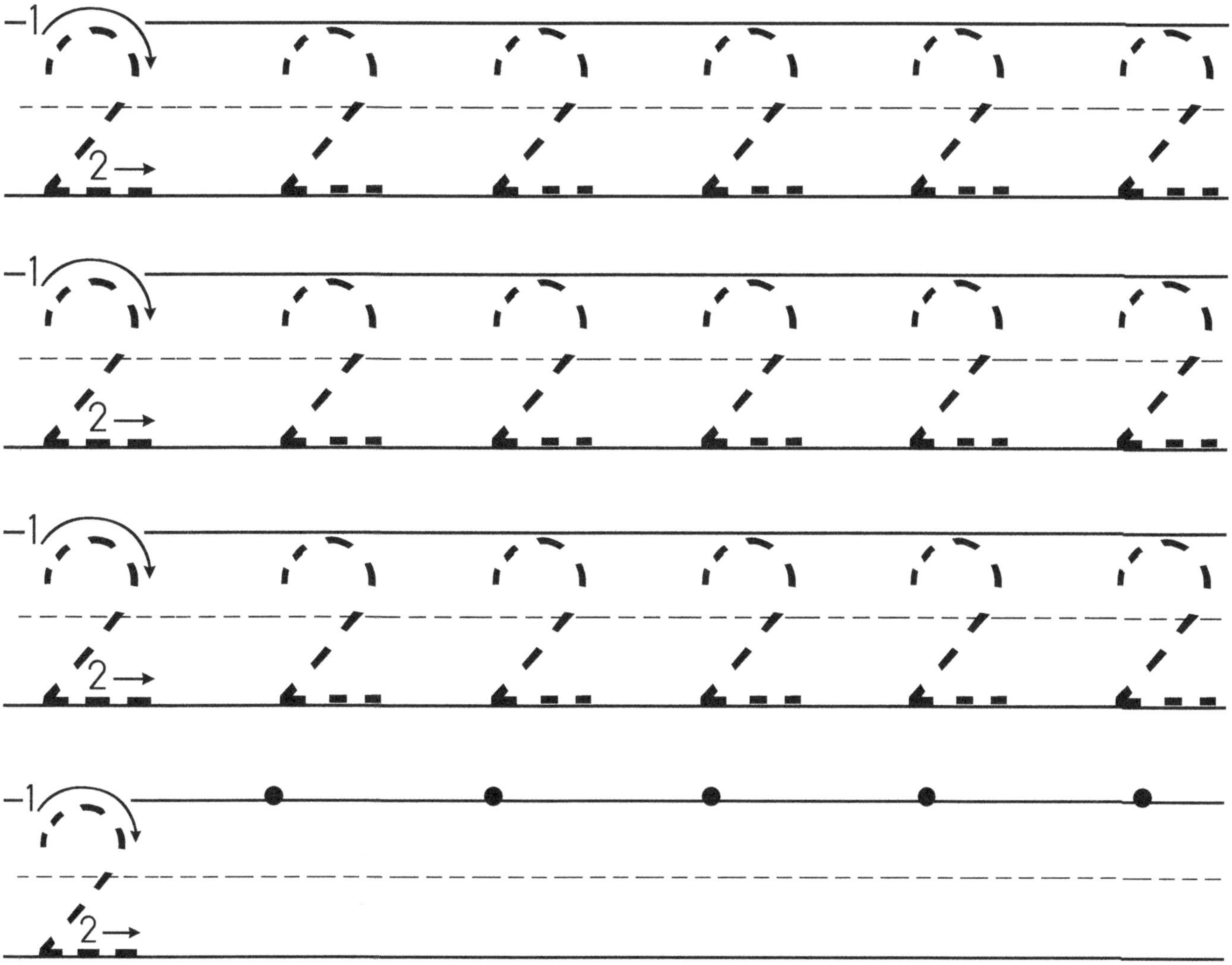

Trace the number. Start at the 1 and follow the numbers and arrows in order.
Color the pictures.

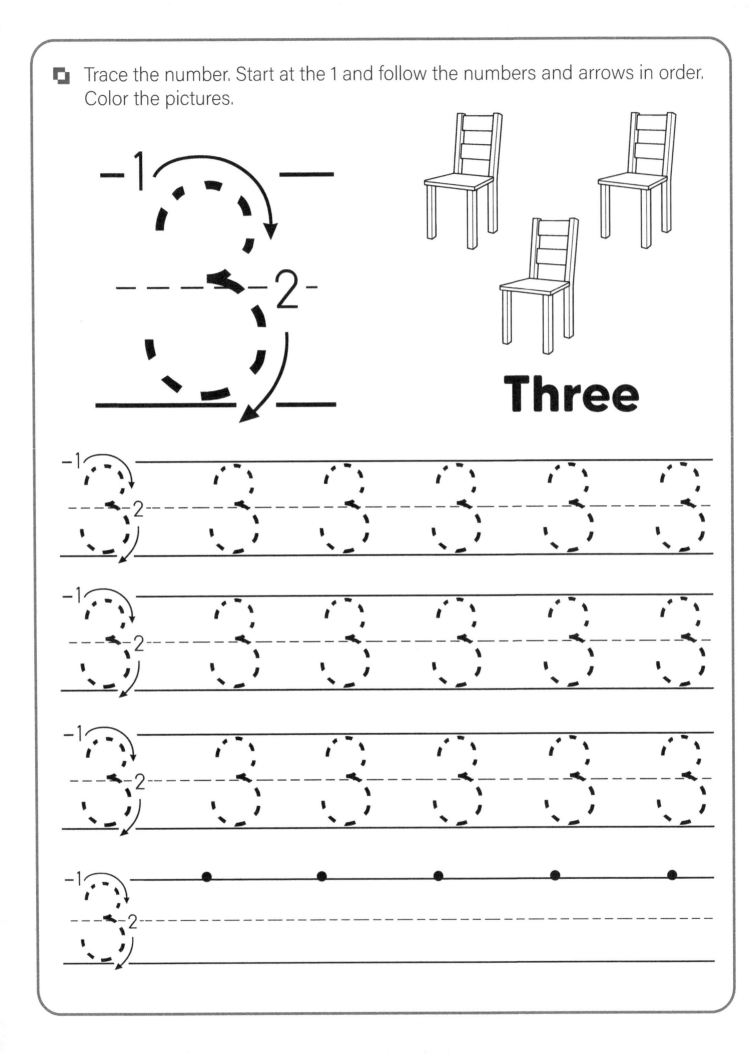

Three

Trace the number. Start at the 1 and follow the numbers and arrows in order. Color the pictures.

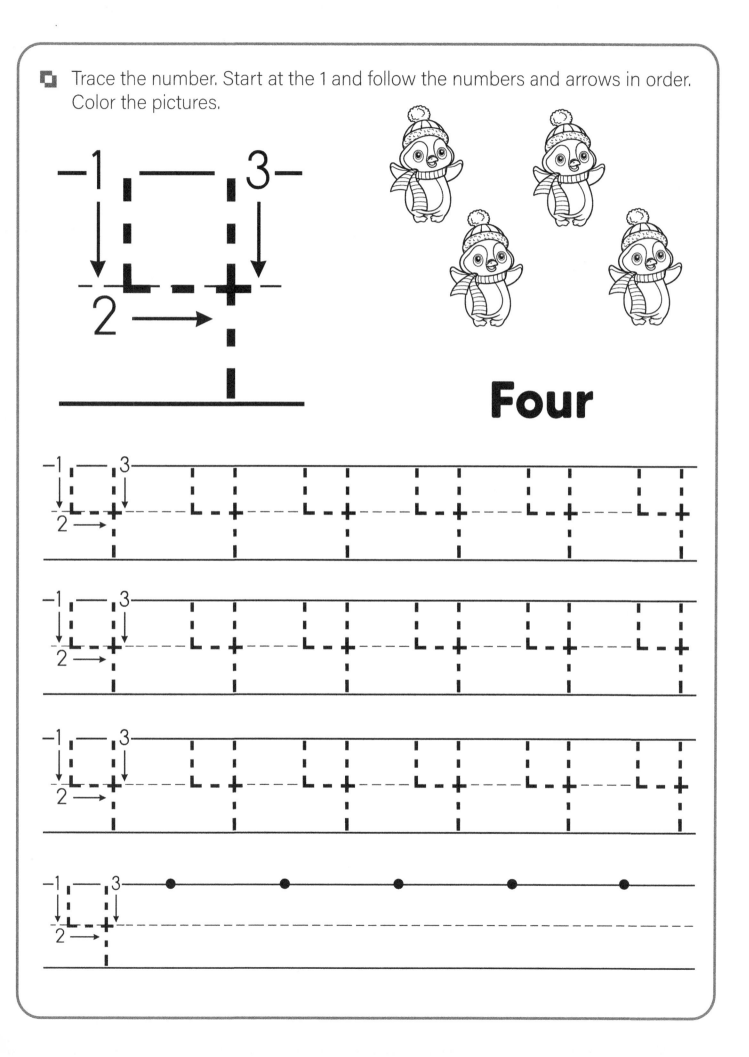

Four

Trace the number. Start at the 1 and follow the numbers and arrows in order. Color the pictures.

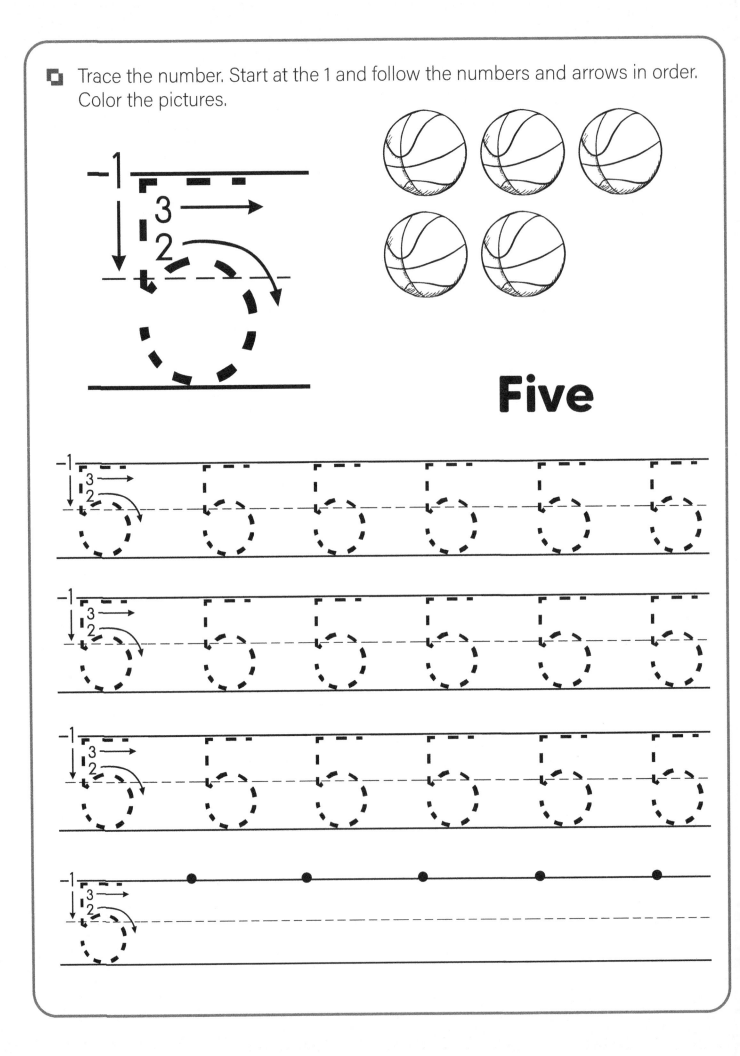

Five

Trace the number. Start at the 1 and follow the numbers and arrows in order. Color the pictures.

1

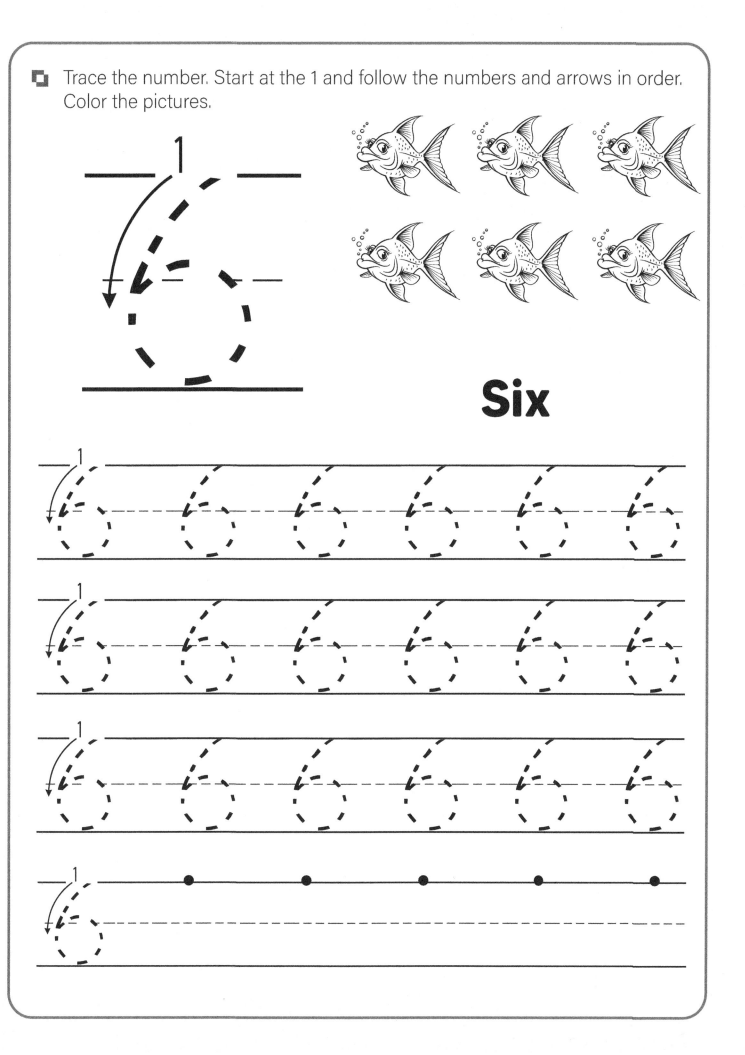

Six

Trace the number. Start at the 1 and follow the numbers and arrows in order. Color the pictures.

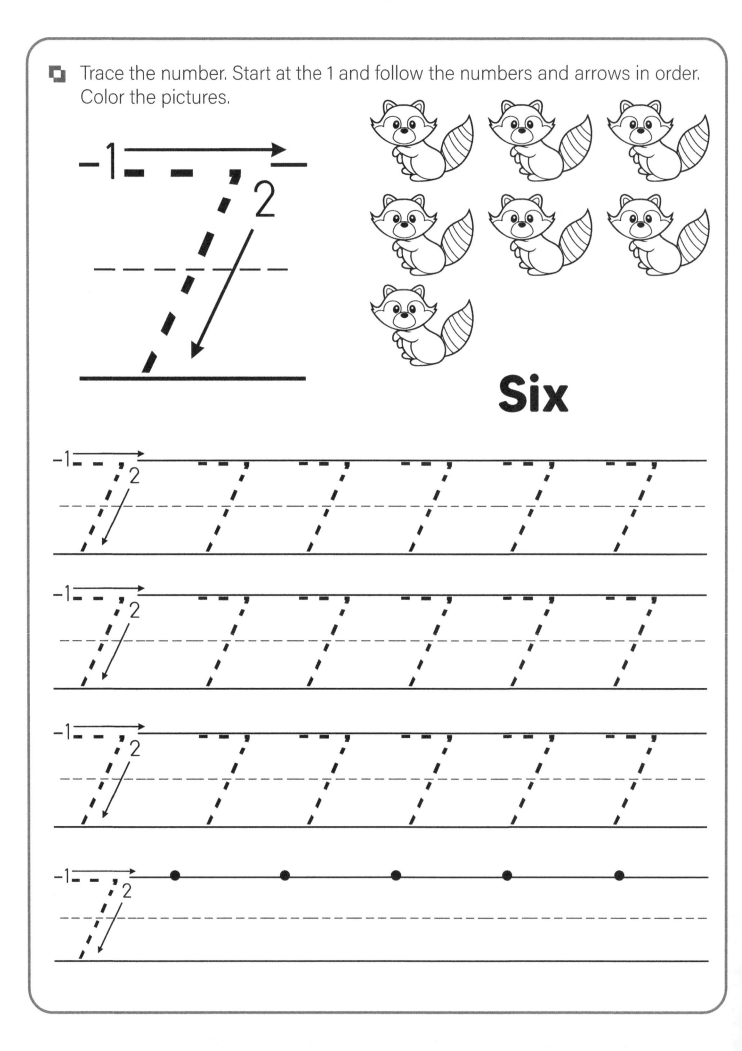

Six

Trace the number. Start at the 1 and follow the numbers and arrows in order. Color the pictures.

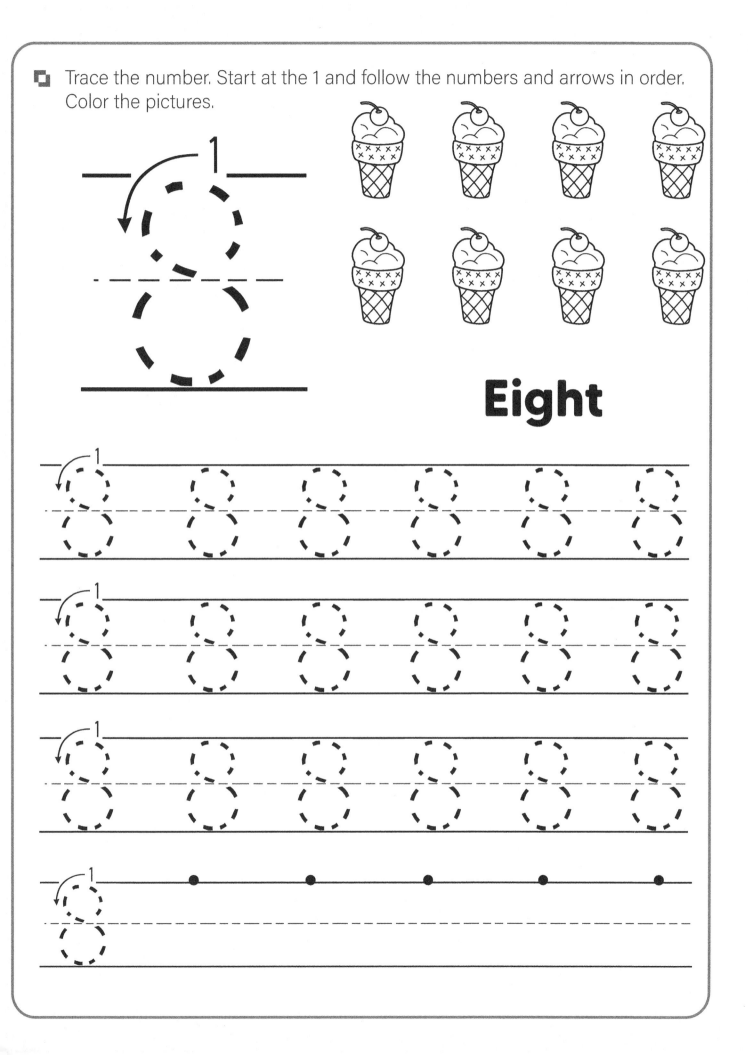

Eight

Trace the number. Start at the 1 and follow the numbers and arrows in order. Color the pictures.

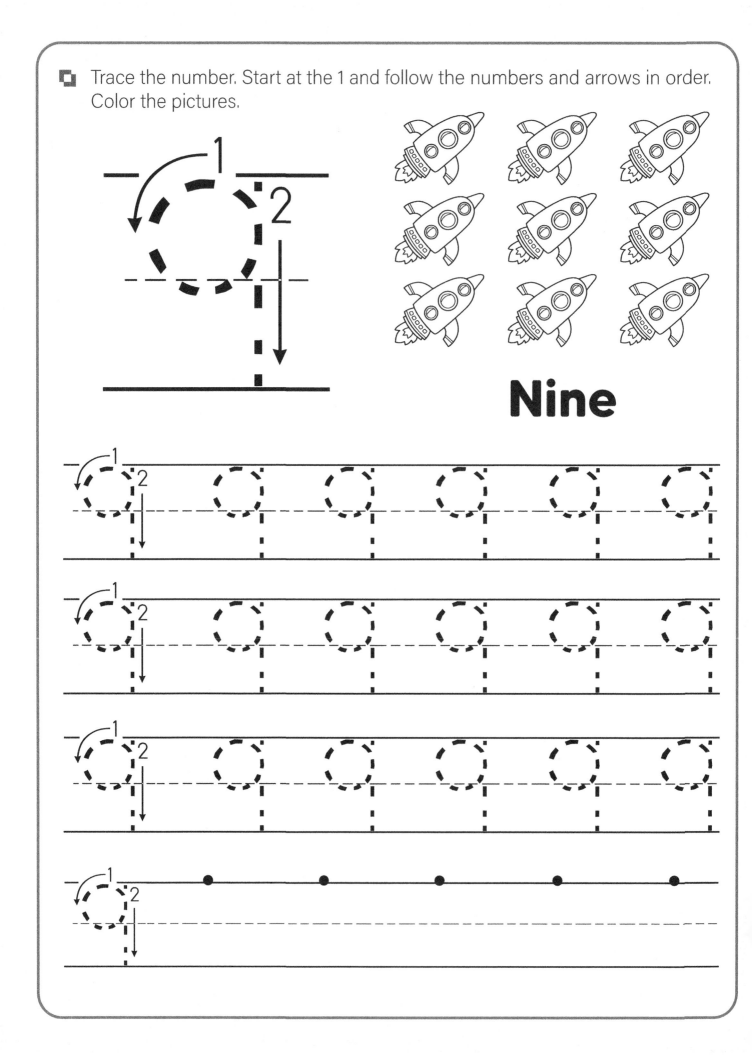

Nine

Trace the number. Start at the 1 and follow the numbers and arrows in order. Color the pictures.

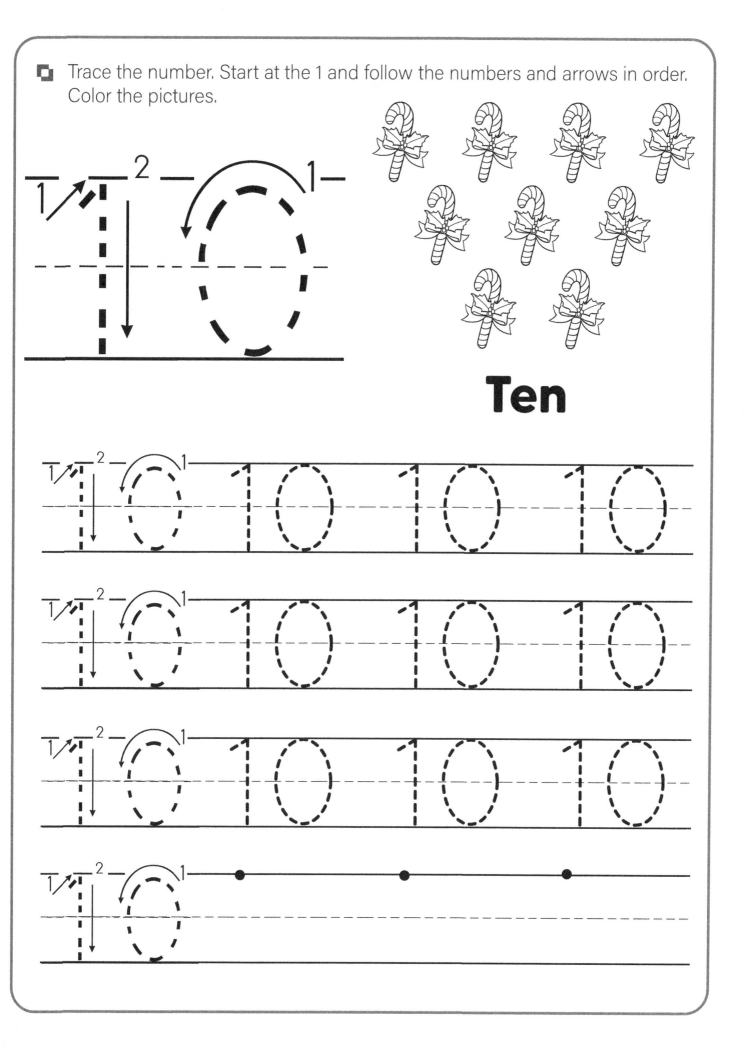

Ten

CIRCLE

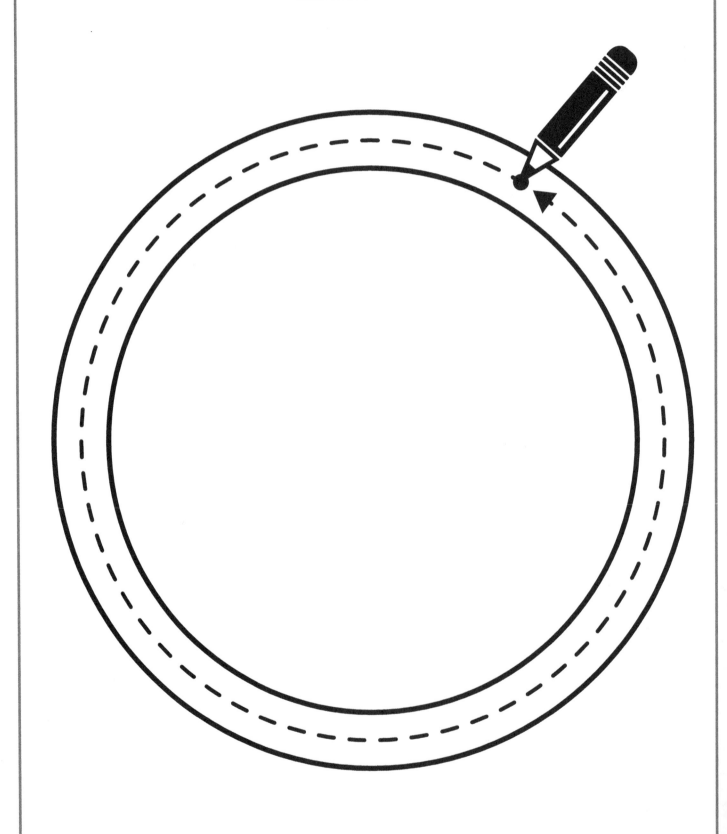

CAR WHEEL

SQUARE

Trace each shape, then color the picture.

Trace each shape, then color the picture.

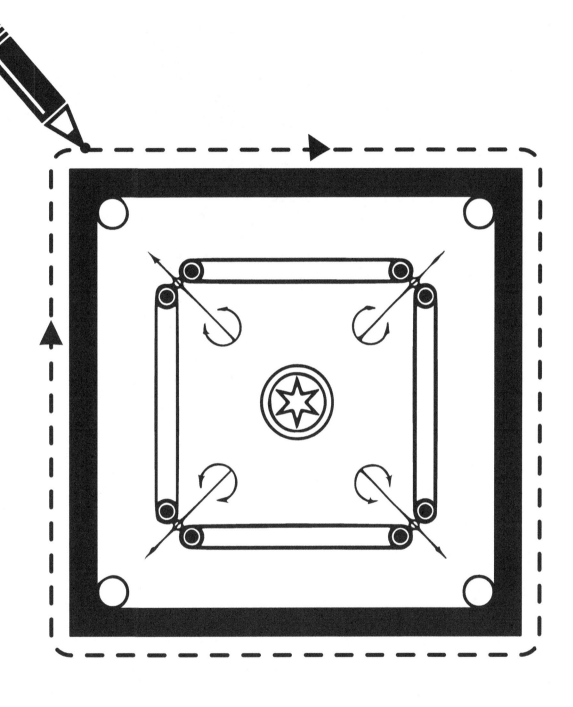

CARROM BOARD

TRIANGLE

Trace each shape, then color the picture.

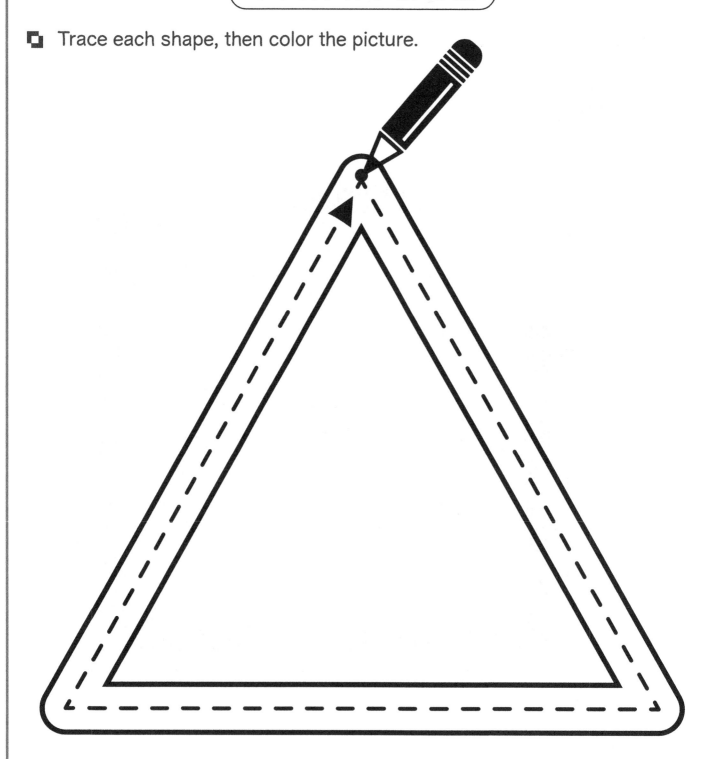

Trace each shape, then color the picture.

PIZZA

OVAL

Trace each shape, then color the picture.

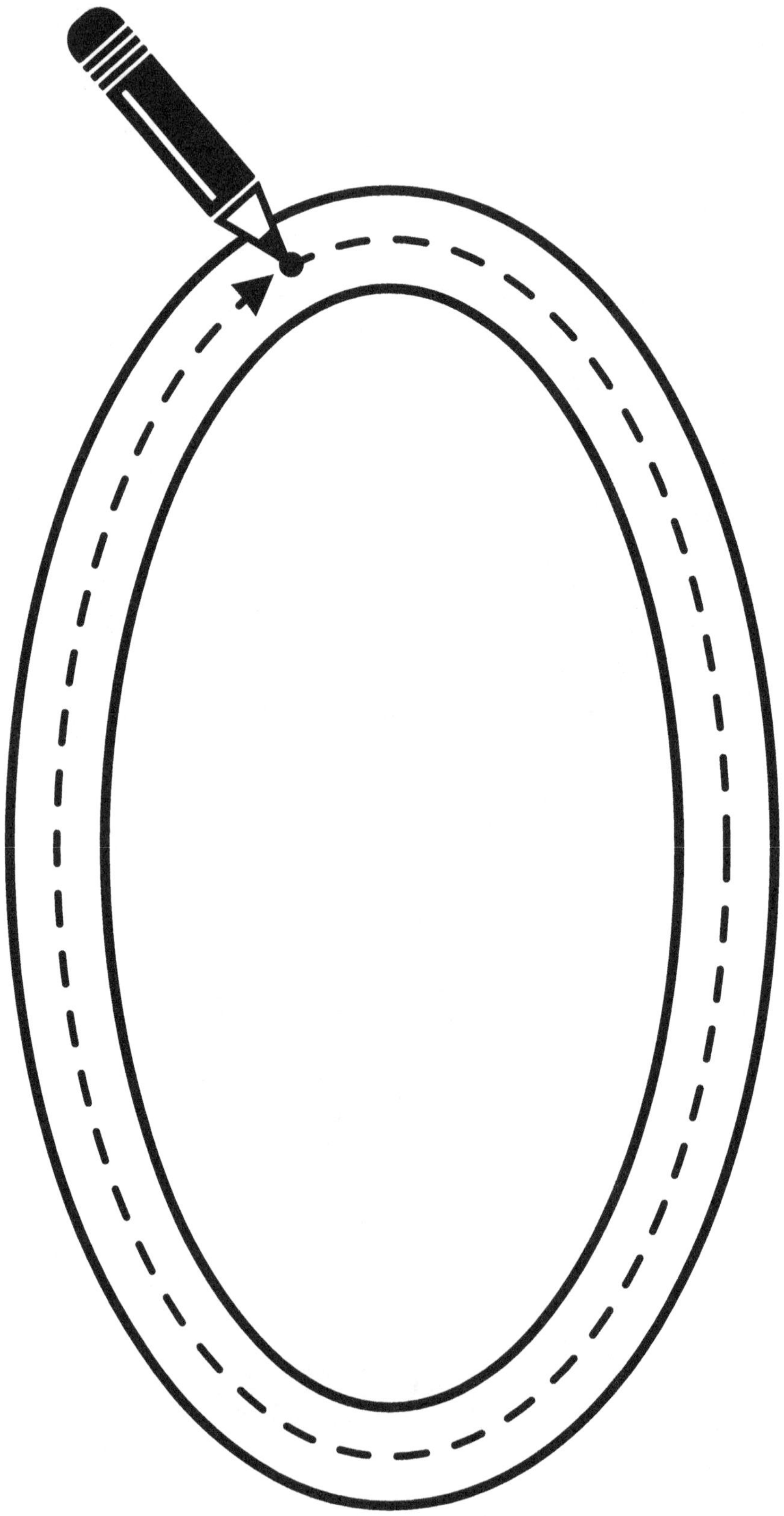

Trace each shape, then color the picture.

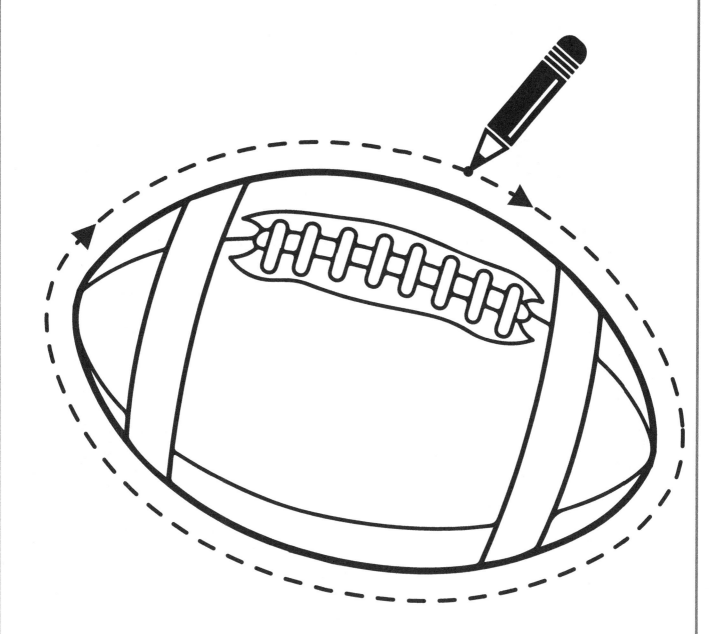

BALL

RECTANGLE

Trace each shape, then color the picture.

Trace each shape, then color the picture.

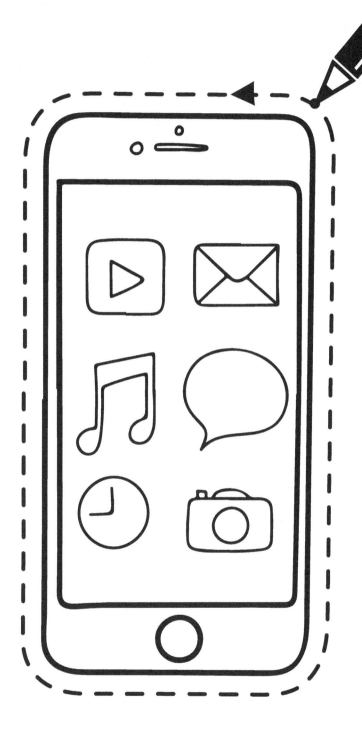

MOBILE

DIAMOND

Trace each shape, then color the picture.

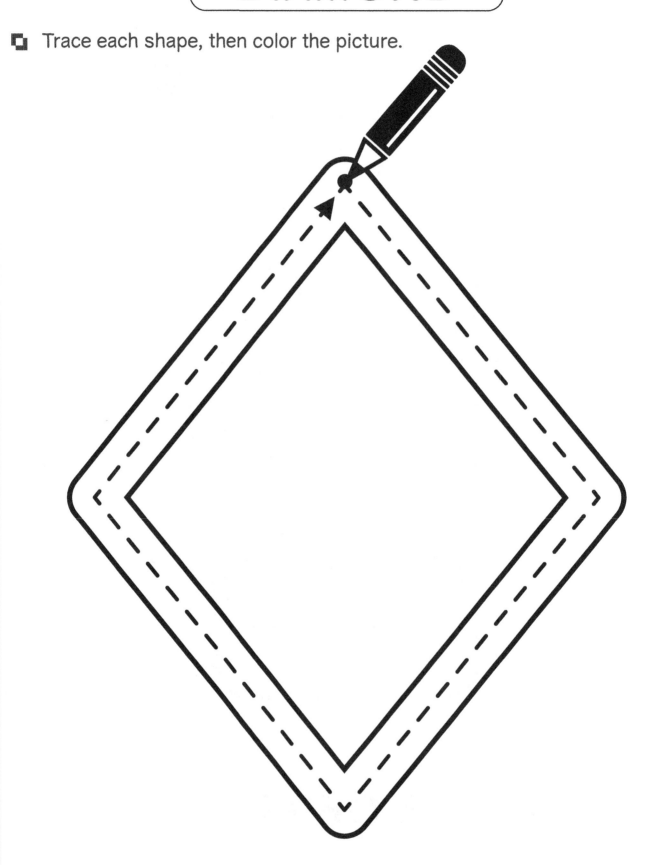

Trace each shape, then color the picture.

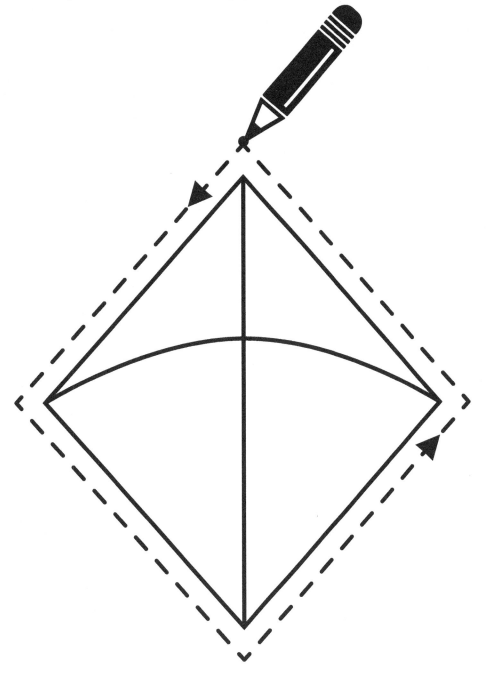

KITE

Trace the word

■ Trace each word.

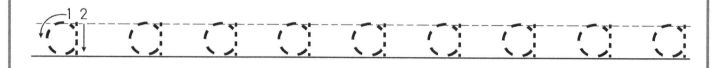

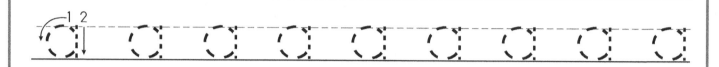

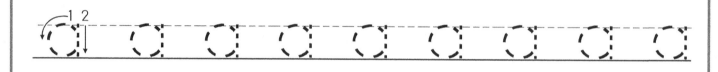

Trace the word

Trace each word.

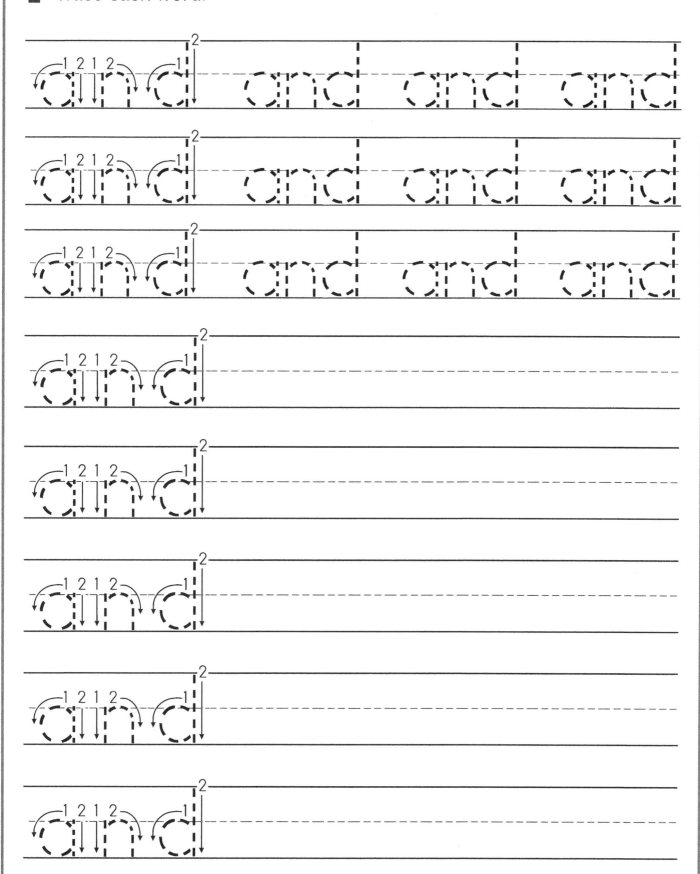

Trace the word

Trace each word.

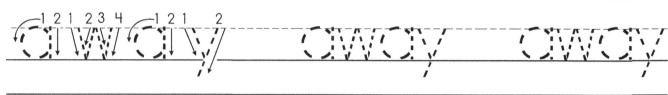

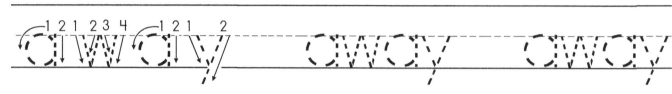

Trace the word

Trace each word.

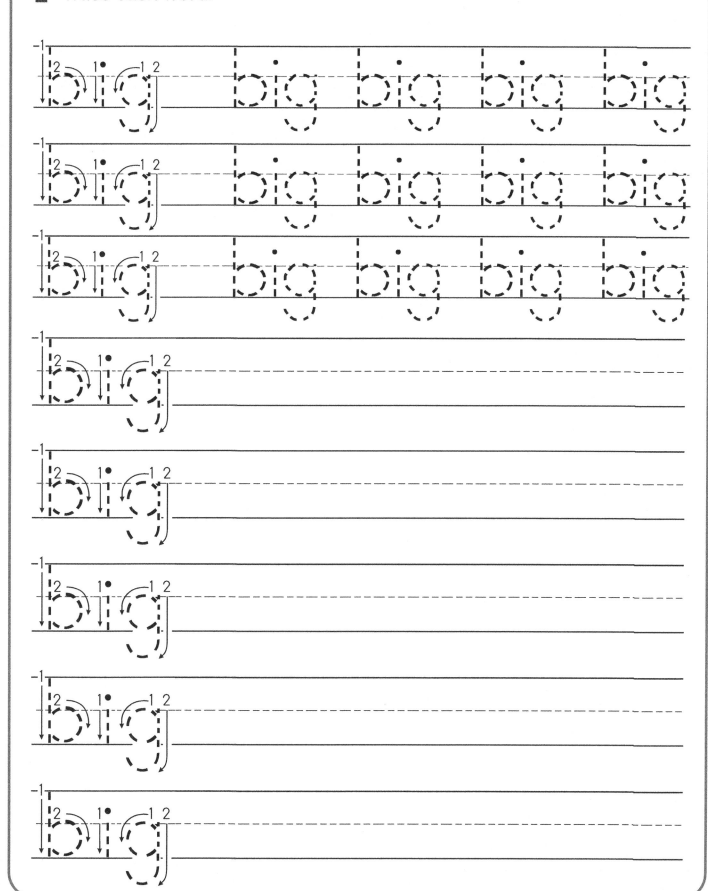

Trace the word

Trace each word.

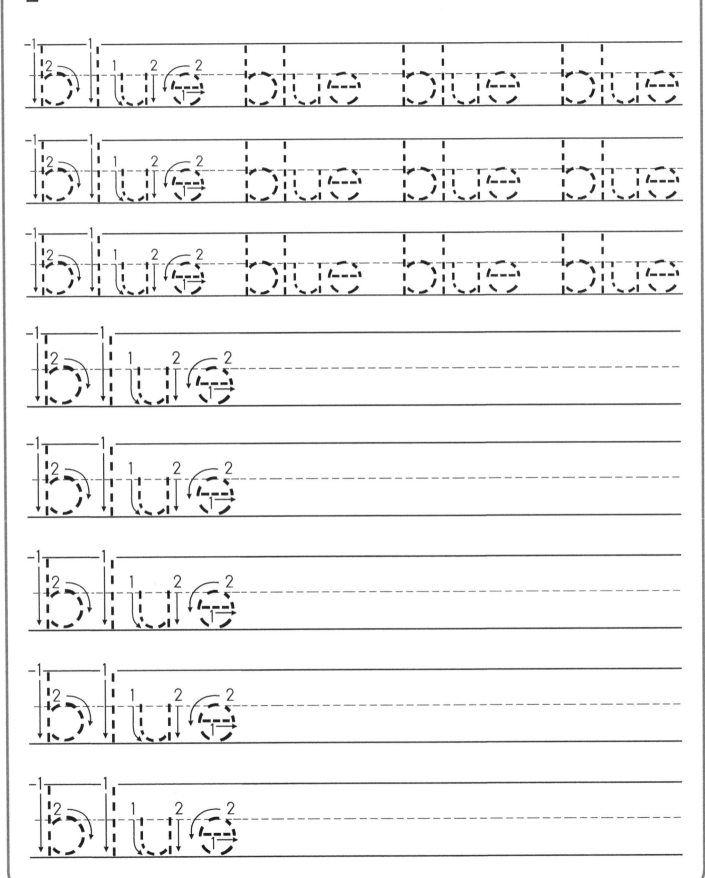

Trace the word

Trace each word.

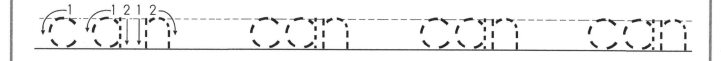

Trace the word

Trace each word.

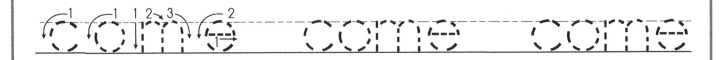

come   come   come

Trace the word

■ Trace each word.

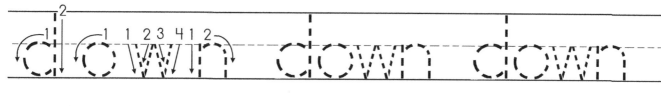

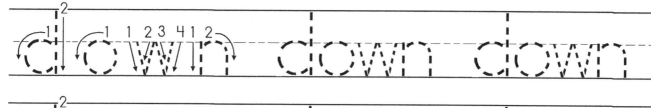

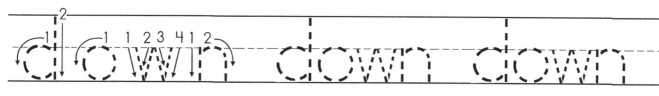

Trace the word

■ Trace each word.

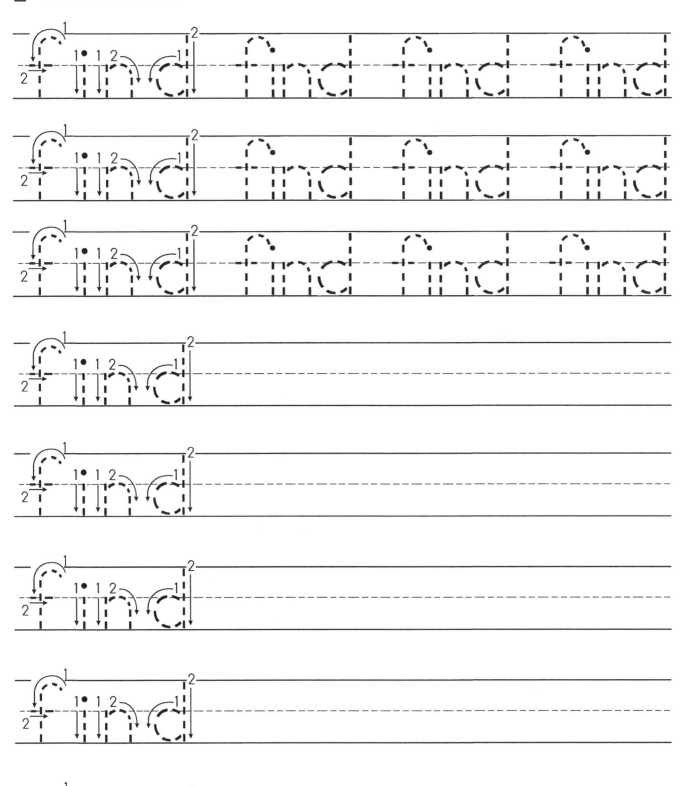

Trace the word

Trace each word.

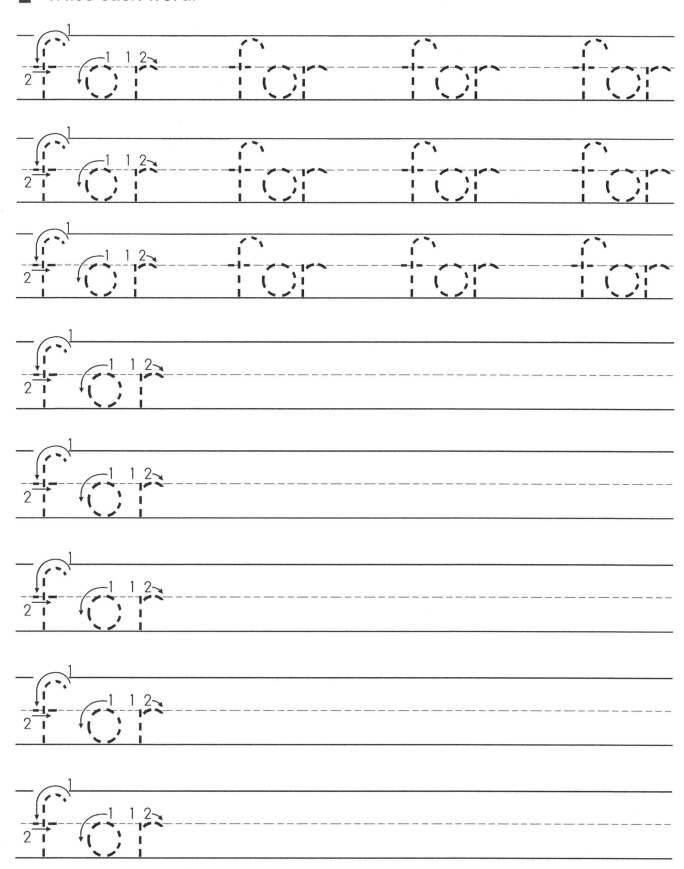

Trace the word

■ Trace each word.

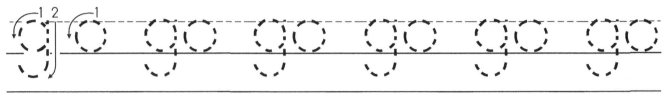

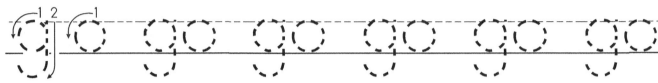

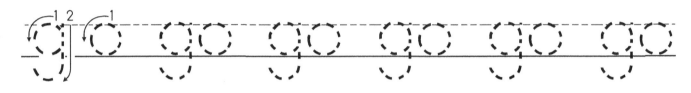

Trace the word

Trace each word.

is is is is is is is is is

is is is is is is is is is

is is is is is is is is is

is

is

is

is

is

Trace the word

Trace each word.

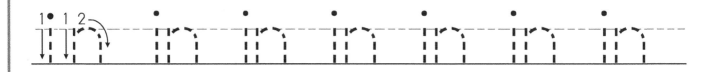

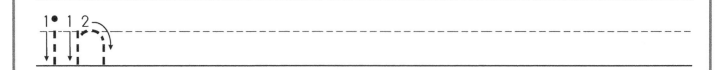

Trace the word

Trace each word.

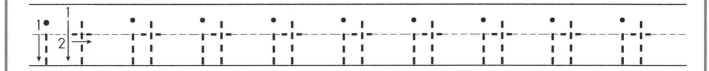

Trace the word

Trace each word.

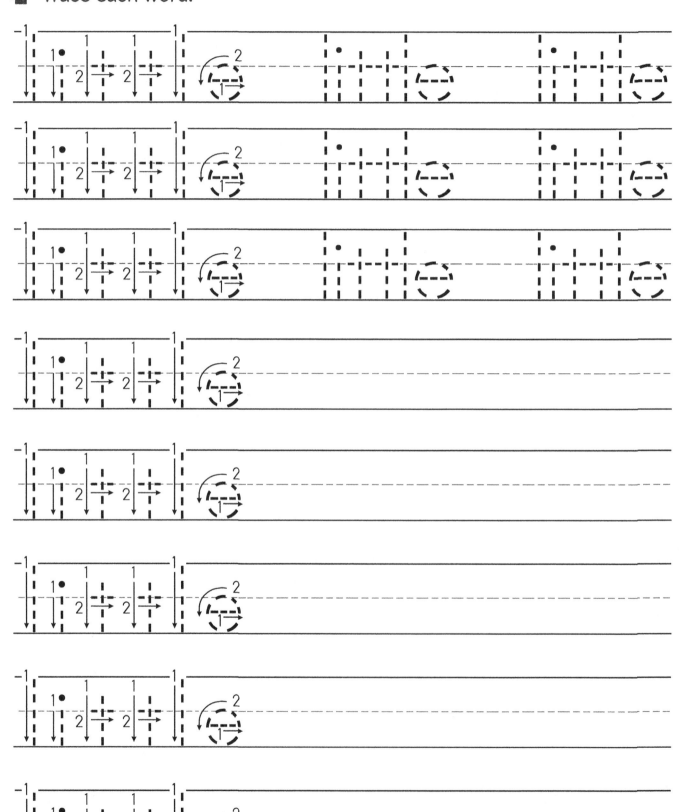

CERTIFICATE

This certificate belongs to:

For learning how to write!

Date _____

Sign up for the FB group of which I am the Unicorn Learning Group administrator. Download all the free materials inside.
You will find resources in digital format ready to print and so much more!

Scan the QR code.

I will see you inside!

Unicorn Learning Group

If this book has met you and your child's expectations, I would appreciate it if you would leave a review on Amazon.

Reviews on Amazon are very important to the goal and work of Unicorn Learning Group as we strive to become providers of quality educational books and resources.

Please log in to your Amazon account, select this book and leave a review.

Also, want to join our emailing list? Email us at unicornlearninggroup@gmail.com put "Unicorn Gems" in the title.

We would love to hear from you and will probably send some goodies your way!

Thanks, A Million!

Unicorn Learning Group

unicorn
LEARNING GROUP

Made in the USA
Middletown, DE
14 October 2022

12754179R00060